# THE BOOK OF
# ALTERNATIVE
# RECORDS

# THE BOOK OF
# ALTERNATIVE
# RECORDS

## PHILIP J. GOULD
## & RALF LAUE

RESEARCHERS: DEAN GOULD & NICK CLAYDON
CONSULTANT: MIKE BARWELL

metro

Published by Metro Publishing Ltd,
3, Bramber Court, 2 Bramber Road,
London W14 9PB, England

www.blake.co.uk

First published in paperback in 2004

ISBN 1 84358 126 4

British Library Cataloguing-in-Publication Data:

A catalogue record for this book is available from the British Library.

Design by www.envydesign.co.uk

Printed in Great Britain by CPD

1 3 5 7 9 10 8 6 4 2

Papers used by Metro Publishing are natural, recyclable products made from
wood grown in sustainable forests. The manufacturing processes conform to
the environmental regulations of the country of origin.

Every attempt has been made to contact the relevant copyright-holders, but
some were unobtainable. We would be grateful if the appropriate people
could contact us.

*Dedicated in love and memory to*
*Violet Joan Gould*

*You have been a source of encouragement,*
*and will always be in our hearts.*

# CONTENTS

# ACKNOWLEDGEMENTS

I wish to extend my gratitude and thanks to the following for their help and encouragement. Without them, this book would not have been possible.

To my wife, Beth Gould, for her support, and for putting up with being alone a good deal of the time over the past year or so.

Darren Staff – for keeping me sane – plus you owe me a tenner!

Unicorn Webdesigners for assistance and support, and for designing our website.

Stuart Ashworth – Press coverage

Richard Cornwell – Press coverage

Record Breakers: Paddy Doyle, Del Lloydo, John Evans, Fred Burton and Creighton Carvello

Adam Gould – thanks for helping with the correspondence

Also, many trhanks to Bob Hattrell, Jonathon Laker, Tony Lazell, Mark Maskell and Mike Sharman.

Special thanks to Lynne Cotton, for your friendship and support over the years. Good luck for whatever you choose to do in the future.

I would like to express my gratitude and thanks to those who helped with the writing of this book, not least of all our research team: Ralf Laue, Dean Gould, Mike Barwell and Nick Clayton. A further word of thanks to Nick, and to Unicorn Web designers for their work on our website, and the assistance given in respect of *Record Holders Republic*.

In addition to the above, I'd like to thank my wife, Beth, for the support and for proof reading the book, and to Darren Staff for his loyal friendship, especially over the past six months when things haven't been quite as rosy.

And to my dear departed Gran, wherever you are now, this book is for you. Thanks for your encouragement and for believing in me.

Philip J. Gould
Ipswich, Suffolk, 19 April 2004

# INTRODUCTION:
## THE AMAZING…

In the fall of 2002 I found myself in the company of my uncle, multi-world record breaker Dean Gould, sharing a laugh over a few beers with my wife and his family. As the night wore on, conversation took a serious turn, and we found ourselves discussing the difficulties record breakers face today in getting recognition for their marvellous feats of dexterity, strength, agility and, in some cases, downright stupidity. Between 1984 and 1990, Mike Barwell had written a book entitled *The Alternative Book of Records*, which was a bizarre collection of weird and wonderful records, and one that Dean recalled captured his imagination and inspired him on to greater record achievements. What we found screaming at us from the back of our minds was the need for a book similar to *The Alternative Book of Records*, but something more relevant, and more comprehensive for today's world. A book that would not only record great human achievement, but inspire others to meet their potential.

On that night many months ago, *The Book of Alternative Records* was conceived, but, before we could give birth to the book, we required the talents of two very special people to help us along the way: Ralf Laue, record breaker and world-record historian, and Mike Barwell – yes, *the* Mike Barwell who wrote *The Alternative Book of Records*. Thankfully, they were both keen.

So, on the back of a chance discussion nearly 22 months ago, we find ourselves here today – at the beginning of a collection of achievable world records. What do I mean by achievable? Well, simply, records that you and I could go out and, theoretically, beat – give or take an ounce of ability and talent! So, you're not going to be reading about the first man who walked on the moon in here, and you won't be finding any information on the largest mammal to walk the earth, either.

This book is for all the amazing people who have ever had a dream, then lived up to the challenge of realising it and achieved the things they once thought beyond their reach. Each and every person within this book has earned their place in history – within these pages are hundreds of record breakers, and we acknowledge them all for being the very best.

# 1

# OUTRAGEOUS
# ACHIEVEMENTS

## AEROPLANE PULLING

Sixty-nine of New Zealand's finest women pulled a Qantas Boeing 737 aeroplane for a distance of more than 100 m (328 ft) at Wellington Airport, New Zealand. Organised by Sue Matson of the Flight Centre at Wellington Airport, the record was set in November 2002.

## AEROPLANE – TAKE-OFFS AND LANDINGS

The most number of take-offs and landings made by a single pilot during a 24-hour period is 308. Walter Mosher, 30, of Blaine, Maine, USA, broke the previous record of 297 that had been set in Australia in 1999 on 23 November 2002 in his three-month-old Cessna 150 aircraft. Because his record-setting flights broke aviation rules, the Federal Aviation Administration revoked his pilot's licence in 2003.

## AIR MATTRESS CHAIN

The longest chain made with air mattresses was formed in Kellenhusen, Germany, and measured 1.2 km (0.745 miles). Approximately 800 people were able to lie across the linked air mattresses.

## ALARM CLOCKS, MOST

The most alarm clocks ever to ring simultaneously rang on 17 April 1999, at exactly 1.00pm in the zoological park of Chomutov, Czech Republic. Try to imagine the noise made by the 520 alarm clocks ringing in unison!

## BACKWARDS TYPING

Jens Seiler, from Germany, typed backwards with a speed of 626 keystrokes per minute on 4 October 1987. He started to train for this record when he had to take part in a beginner's typing course in order to gain a certification. By this time, Jens was already a skilled typist; it's just that he never had the qualification!

## BALLOON BURSTING

Gary Gilbert-Anderson and Mike Taylor, of Leighton Buzzard, Bedfordshire, UK, burst 1,000 air-filled balloons, held in an 2.4 m x 1.8 m (8 ft x 6 ft) container using only hands, feet and body, in the record time of 5 minutes, 33.02 seconds on 18 November 1988 at BBC, Wood Lane Studio, London, for the Children in Need Appeal.

## BALLOON MODELLING

The following records are for making the most balloon animals in a given time:

1 hour: 529 by John Cassidy (USA) in 2003

3 hours: 827 by François Cormier (Canada) in 1991

6 hours: 1,616 by Tip-Top-Till (Germany) in 1999

10 hours: 2,228 by Uwe Lanhardt (Germany) in 1998

24 hours: 6176 by Tim 'The Balloonatic' (USA) in 2004

All balloons have to be blown up by mouth!

The speed record for making 100 dogs from already inflated balloons belongs to Ronald van den Berg (Switzerland) who needed exactly 5 minutes, 48 seconds to twist 100 balloon dogs. This record was established on 24 August 2002 at Sempach, Switzerland.

## BALLOON STUFFING

Ralf Schüler, of Dessau, Germany, managed to squeeze 23 people inside a latex balloon. He also holds a second record for 'going' inside an inflated balloon himself within 37.1 seconds.

## BARGE PULLING

On 23 October 1989, Nathan and John Short pulled a fully laden 150-tonne barge for 500 m (1640 ft) in the record time of 11 minutes, 34 seconds along the quayside at San Francisco, USA.

## BATH OF BAKED BEANS

The longest recorded time for a sit-in in a bath of cold baked beans is 100 hours by Barry (Captain) Kirk of Port Talbot, West Glamorgan, UK. Barry's 'Beanathon' was staged at the Aberfan Hotel between 11 and 15 September 1986.

## BATH OF CUSTARD

Former Army P.T. Instructor, Bill Hammond, 52, of Pickering, North Yorkshire, UK, set a new world record in June 1988 when he sat in a bath full of custard, in a shop window, for 168 hours.

## BATH OF MILK

In true Cleopatra style, 25-year-old Doris Bray, of Sydney, Australia, sat in a bath of milk for 48 hours, from 14 to 15 May 1989.

## BATH OF PORRIDGE

Starting on 1 April 1988, landlord Philip Heard set a new world record of 122 hours, 30 minutes, by sitting in a bath of cold porridge at his pub in Hanam, Bristol, UK.

## BATH PUSHING

The 16 km (10-mile) record for pushing a bath (mounted on wheels) stands at 1 hour, 41 minutes, 44.38 seconds by 3 members of Yateley Hockey Club: Rowan Atkins, Alan Hancock and Giles Hancock (passenger), set on 11 July 1987.

The longest distance that a bath has been pushed in 24 hours is 513 km (318 miles). The feat was achieved by a team of 25 from Tea Tree Gully Baptist Church Adelaide, Australia, from 11 to 12 March 1995.

## BATH OF SPAGHETTI

Rob Gordon, 24, of Shrewsbury, Shropshire, UK, sat in a bath of spaghetti for an incredible 360 hours, starting on 21 September and finishing on 6 October 1984. The bath was mounted on a wheeled trolley so that Rob could be pushed around the streets of Shrewsbury and continue his duties as a disc jockey during the evenings.

## BATHTUB SAILOR

On 9 October 1983, Bill Neal, of Salcombe, Devon, UK, completed a 2900-km (1,800-mile) sail from London to Korkta, Finland, in a fibre-glass Jacuzzi-type bathtub accompanied by 3 friends in a support boat. Bill's journey took almost 4 months to complete.

## BED OF GLASS

The greatest weight held while lying on a bed of glass is 1011.5 kg (2229.95 lb). In April 2002, Rainer Schröder, of Germany, lay on the bed of broken glass with the weight on his body for 10 seconds.

The longest time recorded for lying on a bed of broken glass is 76 hours. Tom Miller, of Australia, carried out this record between 1 April and 4 April 1989.

### WALKING ON GLASS

Sybille Wischgoll (Germany) walked a distance of 843.3 m (922½ yd) in 1 hour at the 7th SAXONIA Record Festival held in Dessau, Germany.

## BED OF NAILS

On BBC Television's *Late, Late Breakfast Show* on 10 December 1983, John Kassar lay prone on a bed of unblunted, 6-in nails. A wooden board was placed on his chest and 29 girls climbed on to it. The total weight pressing down on John's body was 1,650 kg (3,638 lb). Although his body was marked, the sharp nails did not penetrate the skin.

### BED RACING

The longest recorded push of a standard hospital bed in 24 hours is 107.8 km (67 miles, 210 yd), set by a team of 10 (4 pushing and 1 in the bed at a time) from the University of Dublin, Eire, from 23 to 24 September 1989.

### BED OF SWORDS

The longest recorded time for lying across the sharpened blades of four military swords is 36 hours, 10 minutes by Tom Miller, of Fremantle, Australia, from 17 to 18 September 1988.

### BEER MAT TOWER (TALLEST)

Using 76,320 beer mats, a team of 6, all members of a club of brewery collectibles collectors, built a tower of beer mats measuring 14.66 m (48 ft) in height. The tower could have been taller, however, the team had to stop as the ceiling had been reached. This record was achieved by Stephan Carstensen, Burkhard Ohrt, Sascha Janssen, Mark Hirt, Bernd Jensen and Kai Suckow (Germany) within 6 days of starting in April 1994.

### BEER PINT BALANCING

On 15 November 2003, John Evans of Heanor,

Derbyshire, UK, balanced 235 pints of beer on his head, breaking his previously held record of 230.

## BIBLE READING (FASTEST)
Over the Easter period of 1981, 10 youngsters from the Ashby Wesley Methodist Church, Scunthorpe, Humberside, UK, read the entire Bible from the pulpit, covering 773,106 words in the record time of 69 hours, 33 minutes.

## BIBLE WRITING
A group of 6,000 students attending a religious conference in Picarquin, Chile, copied down the Bible by hand in just over 16 minutes. Conference spokesperson Joao Vicente Pereyra said that the students hoped to do better the next year, when they would use only Spanish speaking-students. In the record attempt held in January 2001, 2 Brazilian students slowed them down due to language barriers.

## BODY PAINTING (MASS)
On 10 April 2002, in Leipzig, Germany, 127 body-painted people formed the logo of the Olympic candidate city, Leipzig, for the 2012 Olympic Games.

THE BOOK OF ALTERNATIVE RECORDS

### BRICK CARRYING
Wolfgang Aigner from Innsbruck, Austria, climbed 17 steps of a ladder carrying a backpack containing bricks weighing 172.5 kg (380.29 lb) net. This record was achieved on 14 October 1988.

### BRICK THROWING
At the 'Alternative Olympics' held in Hull, Humberside, UK, on 20 September 1988, Dave Wattle, of Sheffield, UK, threw a 2.268-kg (5-lb) building brick 45.1 m (148 ft, 6 in).

### BROOM BALANCING ON NOSE
Leo Bircher (Switzerland) balanced a broom on his nose for a time of 2 hours, 1 minute.

### BURIAL ALIVE
Geoff Smith, of Mansfield, UK, whose mother, Emma, spent 101 days buried alive in 1968, decided to reclaim the world record held by an American for his mother when he spent 150 days in a specially constructed 0.8 m x 0.8m x 2.1 m (2.5 ft x 2.5 ft x 7ft) coffin. On 29 August 2000, local gravediggers dug a trench in the garden of his favourite pub, The Railway Inn in Mansfield, Nottinghamshire, UK, and buried Geoff 2.1 m (7 ft) under. Having beaten

the world record of 141 days, Geoff was 'resurrected' in January 2001.

## CANNONBALL PUSHING

On 1 March 1986, Reg Morris pushed a cannonball (a 7.3-kg [16-lb] shot) using only his nose, around Walsall, West Midlands, UK, for a distance of 1.6 km (1 mile) in exactly 42 minutes.

Walter Cornelius of Peterborough, UK, took a more arduous route when he pushed a cannonball with his nose along the A6121 at Ketton, Rutland, UK. The course was uphill, but he completed it in 1 hour, 30 minutes!

At the 'Alternative Olympics' held in Hull, Humberside, on 20 September 1988, Pete Dowell of the 'Multex Mentals' team won the 45.7 m (50-yd) cannonball push with the record time of 30.16 seconds.

## CAR CRAMMING

The following car-cramming records show the number of people who managed to squeeze into a vehicle at the same time. These car-cramming records are all subject to the following rules:

• The vehicle must be a standard production model.
• No seats or fitments shall be removed.

- All windows, doors, boot and bonnet must be closed on completion.
- The vehicle's engine must be started on completion of the cram.
- The time limit to achieve the record must be no more than 10 minutes.
- The team members must be aged 16 or above.

*Audi 80:* 21

*British Leyland Metro:* 21, members of the Plymouth Young Wives Association at Davenport, UK, 30 September 1982.

*British Leyland Mini:* 39.

*Ford Escort Mk.1:* 20, students of the Birmingham University, UK, 16 November 1985.

*Ford Sierra:* 27, students at the University of Nottingham, UK, 14 October 1985.

*Mini Cooper:* 21, organised by Fred M at an open-air bath in Plaffenhofen, Germany, 12 July 2003.

*Skoda Felicia:* 28, students of a high school in BMO, Czech Republic, 27 June 1997.

*Skoda Octavia:* 32, students of a high school in BMO, Czech Republic, 27 June 1997.

## OTHER CRAMMING RECORDS

The greatest number of people to cram on to a 56-seater double-decker bus is 354, all pupils from

Churnet View Middle School, Leek, Staffs, UK, 15 December 1989.

The most number of people to cram into a bus designed to transport a capacity of 100 is 358. Made up from students (minimum age of 18) from the neighbourhood of Mlynská dolina, Slovak Republic, participants claimed the record in October 2003, beating the previous record set in July 1998 and held by students of Tamasek Polytecnic, Singapore.

## CAR PULLING – WITH BEARD!

In July 2002, Lithuanian brewer Antanas Kontrimas attached an army jeep (including 5 passengers) weighing almost 3 tonnes to his beard with straps and pulled it for more than 13 m (42.65 ft). Antanas, aged 50, has not shaved for over 25 years and his beard measures more than 50 cm (19.7 in) in length.

## CAR PUSHING

A team from Denmark pushed a Volkswagen car a distance of 10 km (6.2 miles) in a record time of 36 minutes, 18 seconds.

## CATWALK MARATHON

Australian duo Suresh Joachim and Paul Yan broke the World Catwalk distance record of 83.1 miles

13

(133.7 km) when they walked a distance of 84.2 miles (135.5 km) in the fall of 2000. The two record breakers traversed a 16.2-m (53.1-ft) catwalk in Sydney, Australia over 8,364 times in 41 hours to break the original record that had withstood numerous challenges over a period of 17 years. During the distance of over three combined marathons, the Sydney pair also raised awareness and money for the Children's Cancer institute of Australia.

## CAVE DWELLER

The longest period of time that a human has voluntarily remained totally isolated from the rest of civilization is 463 days by the self-styled troglodyte Milutin Veljkovic (Yugoslavia). For scientific purposes, he stood in the Samar cave from 24 June 1969 to 30 September 1970.

## CHERRY STONE SPITTING

*MALE*
Serge Fougère (France) spat a cherry stone a distance of 27.12 m (88.97 ft). He has many similar records, and holds the record for spitting a prune stone a distance of 13.15 m (43.14 ft).

*FEMALE*

The female record for cherry stone spitting is 19.01 m (62.36 ft), held by Conchita Kohler (Switzerland).

## CHRISTMAS TREE BALANCING

David Downes, also known as 'Del Lloydo', of Felixstowe, Suffolk, UK, balanced a 2.1-metre (7-ft) Christmas tree on his chin during the run-up to Christmas in December 2001 for a record-breaking time of 56.82 seconds.

## COAL SACK CARRYING

On 9 November 1990, Paddy Doyle, of Erdington, Birmingham, UK, set the record for the highest number of runs on a 25-m (82-ft) shuttle course while carrying a bag of coal weighing 50 kg (110 lb), when he ran the length of the course 149 times in one hour at the Fox Hollies Leisure Centre in Birmingham.

Fred Burton, from Cheadle, UK, broke the distance world record for carrying a 53.5-kg (117.9-lb) bag of coal around a 25-m (87-ft) course in 20 minutes. During an exhibition at Cheadle's Leisure Centre, Fred carried the bag of coal around the course 114 times, beating the previous record of 91 times.

A team of 8 carried a 45.4-kg (1-cwt) sack of coal a distance of 128.74 km (80 miles) in a record time of 11 hours, 28 minutes, 33 seconds. The men carried the sack of coal around a quarter-mile circuit in Desbury, West Yorkshire, UK, on 20 May 2000. They raised £40,000 for charity in the process.

Ruth Clegg, a 20-year-old student at Liverpool University, UK, broke the women's 1,012.5-m (3321.9-ft) distance record for carrying a 20-kg (44-lb) sack of coal around a course at the World Coal Carrying Championships held in Gawthorpe, NR. Wakefield, West Yorkshire, UK, in the time of 5 minutes, 3 seconds. David Jones, from Meltham, Kirklees, UK, holds the men's world record, which requires a sack of coal weighing 50 kg (110 lb) to be carried over the 1,012.5-m (3321.9-ft) distance. The record time of 4 minutes, 6 seconds was set by David Jones in 1991, and achieved again by the record holder in 1995.

## COCKTAIL MIXING

In 2000, at the 5th Saxonia Record Festival held in Germany, Christian Vögel from Bregenz, Austria, mixed cocktails non-stop for 72 hours, 5 minutes.

## COIN ROTATING

In 1991, Mahendra Singh Rajat, of India, spun two coins alternately for 58 hours, 5 minutes, spinning the second coin before the first fell.

## COLA CAN BALANCING

On 15 November 2003, John Evans, of Heanor, Derbyshire, UK, balanced 428 330-ml cans of coke on his head, beating his previous record of 400 cans. The collective weight of the 428 cans amassed to 171.46 kg (378 lb). The total weight balanced equates to 175 kg (385 lb).

## COMPOSITION

Twentieth-century French composer Erik Satie holds the record for a composition that is the shortest and the longest in the world. 'Vexations' lasts for just under one minute. However, in the score it states that it should be played 840 times in succession – a non-stop playing time of 14 hours.

## COMPUTER GAME PLAYING

The marathon record for playing a computer game was broken when Jürgen Kopmann (Germany) played the computer game 'FATE: Gates of Dawn' for 166 hours in 1991.

## CUE THROWING

The greatest recorded distance that a billiard cue has been thrown, javelin fashion, is 43.10 m (141.4 ft) by Dan Kornblum, in Flensburg, Germany, in 1998.

## DOMINO STACKING

On 28 December 2003, Matthias Aisch of Germany stacked 726 dominoes on top of a single, vertically standing domino. He told the editors of this book that, during practice, he had stacked more than 1000.

## DOMINO TOPPLING

Lead by team leader Robin Paul Weijers, an international team of 90 constructed the world's biggest 'domino course' with four mio dominoes. Weighing a total of 32 tonnes, and using 27 different-coloured dominoes, 3,847,295 of them fell in a chain reaction on 15 November 2002, in Leeuwarden, Netherlands. The dominoes were arranged into 51 'objects' (for example, pictures or a 5-m-tall [16.4-ft-tall] pyramid), and took a time of 92 minutes to collapse in its entirety.

A new solo record for constructing a 'domino course' with 303,621 dominoes was established at the Singapore Expo on 16 August 2003 by Ma Li Hua of China, who for one and a half months, spent

13 hours a day building the giant display. Disaster almost struck during preparations when cockroaches scrambled across the display toppling more than 20,000 dominoes.

## DOMINO BRICK TOPPLING

On 17 January 2004, at the opening of the Weser tunnel in Germany, a brick toppling record was set when approximately 1,500 volunteers built a line of bricks (weighing 2 kg [4.4 lb] each) from Bremerhaven to Nordenham, a distance of almost 27 km (16 miles), and 250,000 bricks were set and toppled successfully. This event was named 'falling stones'.

## EAR WIGGLING – FASTEST

Jitendra Kumar, of Patna, India, can wiggle his ears 147 times in a minute.

## EGG BALANCING

At a world record festival held in Flensburg in July 2002, Dean Gould, of Felixstowe, Suffolk, UK, balanced 13 fresh eggs on the back of a hand, palm down-facing.

## EGG FRYING

Using the same single frying pan, a team of six housewives led by Eileen Adams, 55, of Powys, Wales, UK, set a world record at the British Gas Kitchen Centre, London, UK, by frying 8,731 eggs in 192 hours.

## EGG WALKING

Volkmar Koch, of Germany, whose weight is 80 kg (176 lb), set the record for walking on uncooked hen's eggs. While wearing special shoes (his son's roller skates adapted for the record attempt), and with ten fresh hen's eggs under each shoe, Volkmar managed to take 16 steps before an egg broke.

## ELECTION – THE SMALLEST TURNOUT

Nil. In 1991, the people of a town in Krasnopol, Poland, stayed at home in force in the election for a new mayor. Not even the two candidates turned out!

## ELEVATOR CAPTIVE

Armando Piazza, of Sestriere, Italy, survived for 10 days in a lift without food or water during 1988. He stepped on the scales afterwards 14 kg (31 lb) lighter weighting 86 kg (190 lb).

## FAN OF CARDS

Ralf Laue of Germany held a fan of 326 playing cards in one hand in Leipzig, Germany on 18 March 1994. The value and colour of each card was clearly visible on one side of the card, and no adhesives were used.

## FERRET LEGGING

The undisputed world Ferret Legging Champion was 78-year-old Reg Mellor (d. 1987) of Barnsley, Yorkshire, UK, Indeed, Reg claimed to be the originator of this 'sport' when, as a boy of eight, he used to keep his hunting ferrets warm and dry by stuffing them down his trousers after a day in the fields. On 5 July 1981, at the Annual Pennine Show at Holmfirth, Yorkshire, Reg broke his own world records by keeping two live ferrets down his trousers for a time of 5 hours, 26 minutes. Reg performed the feat in front of over 5,000 people and, although badly bitten in 'all the wrong places', he persevered to the bitter end.

N.B. During record attempts, no undergarments can be worn, and the trouser bottoms must be firmly secured with string.

### FIGHTING IN ARMOUR

Wearing full weight (27.2 kg [60 lb]) armour and using 4.5 kg (10-lb) swords, Stephen Thomas and Khrys Yuen of the York Company of Knights performed 9.5 sets (each set is 6 strokes) in 2 minutes while fighting at Patrington Haven, Humberside, UK, on 13 July 1986.

### FIRE WALKING

Sixteen people from Switzerland, aged from 15 to 58, took part in the longest fire walk in history on 15 March 2003 when they walked over burning wood a distance of 222 m (728 ft). This event was organised by Dream Factory, Thierachern, Switzerland.

### FLYING WITH BALLOONS

In 1998, John Ninomya (USA) broke the record for a flight powered by a cluster of balloons. Ninomya floated to a height of 21,400-ft beating the previous record of 11,000ft.

The British record is 18,235 ft by Mike Howard and Steve Davis, achieved during 2001. The balloons used for both records were bigger than the usual 'toy balloons' or 'party balloons'.

## FOOTBALL FAN PHOTOGRAPHY

Aston Villa fan Tom Gill, a 13-year-old football-mad schoolboy, has amassed a collection of more than 500 photographs taken of himself with different soccer stars. Starting when he was just ten, Tom has 27 photo albums full of pictures that include England stars David Beckham, Alan Shearer, Glen Hoddle and World Cup match-winning goal scorer Geoff Hurst.

## GRAPE CATCHING

*SPEED*

The most grapes thrown over a distance of 15 ft, and caught in the mouth in one minute is 55, by Steve Spalding (USA). It was performed at Grapefest in Grapevine, Texas on 14 September 2002. The thrower was Scott Spalding.

Steve Spalding also holds the record for 30 minutes, catching 1,189 grapes during this time.

*HEIGHT*

The greatest height from which a grape has been dropped from a moving aircraft (in this case a balloon) and caught in the mouth is 9.15 m (30 ft) by Peter Tilney (dropper) and Tony Gough (catcher) on 25 July 1985. The pair had aimed for greater heights, but were foiled by a thick mist rising from the River Severn at Attringham Park, Shrewsbury, Shropshire, UK.

### SOLO – THROW, RUN AND CATCH
The solo grape-catching record belongs to Camilo Antonio Mendez, UK. He caught a grape in his mouth thrown a distance of 12.05 m (39 ft 6 in).

## GUIDED CITY TOUR
The world's longest guided city tour took place on 21–22 June 2003 in Augsburg, Germany. Of 33 tourists who started the tour, 21 completed it visiting museums, rivers, towers, etc. for a total time of 33 hours, 24 minutes. The participants listened to nearly 100 city guides who worked in shifts.

## GUM WRAPPER CHAIN
Gary Duschl, of Virginia Beach, Virginia, USA, holds the record for the longest gum wrapper chain in the world. In June 2004, the chain contained 1,036,574 gum wrappers, and had a length of 13,526 m (44,378 feet). It would take 3 hours to walk the chain's length, or 8 minutes by car travelling at a speed of 101 k/h (63 mph). It contains $51,778.70 worth of gum. Gary started the chain on 11 March 1965.

## HITCH-HIKERS

The record for the most number of hitch-hikers a driver has given a ride to goes to Dieter Wesch of Germany. He has had 9,500 hitch-hikers in his car. Each of them has signed his 'guest book'. Dieter does not wait for people who are searching for a hike, instead he searches for hitch-hikers himself at petrol stations, etc.

## HOPPING, FASTEST MILE

Tony Murray, 19, of Leicester, UK, hopped on one leg for a distance of 1 mile around the track of Loughborough College in the record time of 29 minutes, 11.4 seconds on 19 September 1989.

## HORSEBACK RIDING, WITH 2 HORSES

The longest horseback ride with 2 horses (the one which was not ridden carried the luggage), was achieved in 1926 by Professor Aimé Tschiffely of Switzerland, who travelled from Buenos Aires, Argentina to New York, USA – a distance of 21,500 km (13,360 miles). Using his horses, Mancha (aged 15) and Gato (aged 16), he had to cross a mountain of 6,000 m (19685 ft), and tolerate temperatures of 48°C as they travelled through a desert.

## HOT WATER BOTTLE BURSTING

On 26 October 2003, the record for bursting a British Standard hot water bottle is 35.6 seconds by Fred Burton at The Winking Man nightclub, near Leek, Staffordshire, UK.

The record for arbitrary hot water bottles is 8 seconds, achieved by 14-year-old Vijay Kumar Bansfore of India on 4 June 2002 in New Delhi, India.

## HOUSE BRICK BALANCING

The largest number of house bricks ever to be balanced on the head is 101, a record held by John Evans, of Heanor, Derbyshire, UK. John has held this balancing record since 1994, and broke this record no less than four times before settling for the current record of 101, achieved on BBC's National Lottery television programme on 24 December 1997.

## HULA-HOOP

*MOST*

The greatest number of hula-hoops spun was achieved on 26 April 2004 by Aleysa Goulevich (Belarus). She managed to spin 100 hoops simultaneously on her body.

## *THE LARGEST*
Paul Blair (USA) rotated a giant hoop (circumference 13.2 m [43.3 ft]) around his waist in June 2003 in Bellevue, Washington, USA.

## *RUNNING*
Roman Schedler, of Austria, ran 100 m (328 ft) while spinning a hoop in a time of 13.84 sec on 16 July 1994.

Paul Blair, of USA, ran 1 mile while spinning a hoop in 7 minutes, 47 seconds. He also walked 10 km (6.2 miles) while spinning a hoop in a time of 1 hour, 6 minutes, 35 seconds.

## **HULA-HOOP WITH A TRACTOR TYRE**
Roman Schedler, of Austria, spun a tractor tyre weighing 24 kg (53 lb) for 71 seconds at the 5th Saxonia Record festival on 24 September 2000 in Bregenz, Austria.

## **ICE BALL STACKING**
Gianni Mucignat, of Germany, an owner of an ice café, holds the world record for stacking ice balls. He stacked 539 ice balls (weighing 17 kg [37.5 lb]) on one waffle in 1990.

## INLINE SKATES

The fastest anyone has been pulled behind a motorcycle while wearing inline skates is 291.8 km/h (181.3 mph). Dirk Auer, of Germany, used specially constructed inline skates for the record attempt, and set the record on 11 August 2002 near Darmstadt, Germany. Behind a car (a Porsche sports car), Dirk was even faster, recording a speed of 307.4 km/h (191 mph), which he achieved in 1999.

## INTERNET CHAT

The record for the longest Internet chat belongs to a team of Austrian chatters from 'energy.at'. From 4 to 8 September 2001, they had a chatting session lasting 104 hours, 12 minutes.

## IRONING BOARD BALANCING

On 9 December 2003 at the Henley Road Cricket Stadium, Ipswich, UK, balancing multi-record breaker Del Lloydo (a.k.a. David Downes) set the world record for balancing an ironing board in the open position on his chin for a time of 3 minutes, 32 seconds.

## KITCHEN SINK BALANCING

In Ipswich, Suffolk, UK, in February 2002,

Felixstowe man Del Lloydo (a.k.a. David Downes) set a record by balancing a 4.9 kg (10 lb 8 oz) kitchen sink on his chin for a time of 1 minute, 9 seconds.

## LADDER STILT WALKING

In October 2001, David Downes, of Felixstowe, Suffolk, UK, 'stilt' walked using two 7-ft ladders a distance of 20 m (65 ft).

## LEGO TOWER

The tallest LEGO tower ever constructed was built using 500,000 LEGO bricks, and measured a height of more than 27.4 m (90 ft). This record was set between 12 and 16 February 2004 at Legoland, California, USA.

## LETTER OPENING

Ralf Laue of Germany opened 1,000 letters in the world record time of 29 minutes, 3 seconds on 14 July 1996 in a letter-opening contest held in Germany.

## LOG CARRYING

Fred Burton, of Cheadle, Staffordshire, UK, carried 100 logs one at a time weighing 25 kg (55.1 lb) over a 10-m (32.8-ft) course in 16 minutes, 42.73 seconds in November 1995.

Super-fit Paddy Doyle, of Erdington, Birmingham, UK, set the record for carrying a 25.4 kg. (56 lb) log over a distance of 7.6 m (25 ft) when he completed the distance 100 times in 21 minutes, 40 seconds on 31 October 1994 at Cannon Hill Park, Birmingham.

## MARRIAGE – MOST REJECTIONS

In 1976, Keith Redman asked his future wife, Beverley on her 16th birthday whether she would marry him for the first time. She said 'no', as she did on a further 8,800 occasions during the next 14 years. However, at the age of 39, she finally agreed to marry him.

## MARRIAGE VOWS, MOST

Lauren and David Blair of the USA first got married on 6 May 1984. Since then, they have renewed their wedding vows 83 times (up to October 2004) at different venues, such as on a stage at a theatre after a performance of Romeo and Juliet and at London's Hard Rock Café.

## MATCHSTICK STACKING

This record requires that the matchsticks are stacked on a bottle neck. In 2002, Peter Both, of Rostock, Germany, stacked 10,000 matches without using any adhesive.

## MATCHSTICKS – BURNING IN A CHAIN REACTION

562,167 matches on a 4-m (13.1-ft) tower were burnt in a chain reaction, taking 34 minutes in the record attempt held in Hückeswagen, Germany.

## MILK CRATE BALANCING ON HEAD

John Evans, of Heanor, Derbyshire, UK, holds the record for balancing the most milk crates on his head. On 6 April 2001, John performed this feat in Hyde Park, London, and balanced a record breaking 96 crates.

## MINIATURE STEAM LOCOMOTIVE

On 11 January 1998, the record for the non-stop running of a model steam locomotive was broken when a team from Japan smashed the record after 36 hours of non-stop motion. The driver team of 8 took it in turns to sit on the little engine as it went around the track 717 times at the Exhibition Centre in Sinsheim, Germany – all without stopping. The total distance travelled was 215.1 km (133.66 miles), which calculates to an average speed of 5.98 km/h (3.72 mph).

## MODEL LOCOMOTIVE

The heaviest locomotive pulled by model train locomotives weighed 86 tonnes, and was pulled over a distance of 6 m (19.68 ft) in Munich, Germany in 1996 by 86 model locomotives made by the manufacturer Roco of Austria.

## MODEL RAILWAY TRAIN

The longest model railway train consisted of 2,108 vans, which were pulled by 10 locomotives over a distance of 35.14 m (115.28 ft). The attempt was part of the International Model Railway Exhibition held on 1 November 1993 in Stuttgart, Germany, and the whole train measured a length of 242.42 m (795.33 ft).

## MOTIONLESSNESS

Akshinthala Seshu Babu, of India, stood motionless in Mahatma Gandhi's posture with a stick for the world record with a time of 25 hours, 1 minute in 2001 and for 35 hours in 2002. Another record of 30 hours, 12 minutes in 2003 was achieved without a stick.

## MOUNT EVEREST CLIMBING

To commemorate the 50th anniversary of Sir Edmund Hillary's Everest expedition, mountaineers set a number of new world records during the first half of 2003, including:

*The world's oldest summitter:* Japanese ski instructor Yuichiro Miura is the oldest climber ever to reach Mount Everest's summit. He was 70 years and 222 days old when he reached the summit.

*The world's youngest summitter:* 15-year-old Sherpa girl Mingkipa is the youngest climber ever to reach the summit of Mount Everest.

*The world's fastest summitter:*
Pemba Dorji Sherpa (Nepal) 'raced' from the 5297.4 m (17,380 ft) base camp to Everest's summit in a record 8 hours, 10 minutes in May 2004. The usual journey time takes approximately 4 days.

## NAILS – MOST HAMMERED BY HAND
On 2 October 1999, Chu-Tan-Cuong of Germany, used his hand to drive 116 nails into a wooden board in a time of 11 minutes.

## NAIL STACKING
For this record, the first nail (which must be 100 mm long) is placed in a vertical position into a piece of wood. On top of this vertical nail the other nails are

carefully placed. No nails must touch the piece of wood or the table. The current record is held by Ralf Laue, Germany, who stacked 115 nails on top of a single vertical one on 20 June 2003 in Pelhrimov, Czech Republic.

## OIL LAMPS

The highest number of oil lamps lighted on one occasion is 30,000 at the lantern festival in Malacca, Malaysia, on 3 September 2000.

## PANCAKE TOSSING

The record for the most flips of a pancake in a frying pan (8½ inch base measurement) in 2 minutes is 416 flips, held by Ralf Laue of Germany.

The highest a pancake has been tossed and re-caught in the pan is 8.60 m (28.21 ft) over a bar by Jean-Marie Livonnen of France.

## PAPERCLIP CHAINS

The longest paperclip chain constructed by a single person was made by Thomas Paul (Germany) in 1992. His 250-m-long (8,202-ft-long) chain was made from 111,000 paperclips. For his attempt, he used the holiday from school.

On 13 February 2004, Dan Meyer (USA) with

the help of some 25 clip-pushers and spool-spinners assembled a 1,629-m-long (5,340-ft-long) paperclip chain, using 54,030 paperclips in the process – the longest constructed by a single person in 24 hours.

## PAPER SHIPS FLOATED

The record for the largest number of paper ships ever floated on water belongs to Markus Kunz of Germany. Taking 432 working hours, Markus folded 13,131 paper ships, and then set them to float on 6 September 1980 in water at a swimming pool in Landau, Germany. To qualify, all the paper ships need to be floating at the same venue, and at the same time.

The record for folding the most paper ships in general goes to Peter Koppen of Munich, Germany. He has folded more than 200,000 of them. Koppen arranges them in colourful images and sells the collages as artwork.

## PAPER PLATE THROWING

On 10 August 1990, Alan Thomas, of Yeovil, Somerset, UK, set a new world record for paper plate throwing, when he achieved a distance of 15.48 m (50 ft 8 in) without the aid of wind assistance.

## PEA PUSHING

Using only the nose and with fresh peas, the current records for pushing a pea are:

*100 yards* in 4 minutes, 30 seconds by Helen McDonald, of Derby, UK, on 14 February 1970.

*1 mile* in 6 hours, 40 minutes by Helen McDonald, of Derby, UK, on 14 February 1970.

*2 miles* in 15 hours, 28 minutes by Helga Jansens, of Peterborough, Cambridgeshire, UK, on 15 August 1978.

The longest distance a pea has ever been pushed is 2 miles, 50 yd by Alex Crawford, 23, on 3 September 1978, at Peterborough, Cambridgeshire, UK, in a time of 16 hours exactly.

## PEANUT PUSHING

Using only his nose, Mark McGowan, of Peckham, south-east London, UK, set the distance record for pushing a monkey nut in an attempt to wipe out his student debts. Starting at Goldsmiths College in New cross, south-east London, and finishing at 10 Downing Street, Mark began the 11.3-km (7-mile) distance on 1 September 2003 and finished the journey on his hands and knees on 12 September 2003.

## PEDAL CAR JOURNEY

Manfred Klauda of Germany, who has the world's largest collection of children's pedal cars (450 in own museum), travelled a distance of 4,588 km (2,851 miles) from Munich to Dresden. The record in this category must be performed in a pedal car originally built for children.

## PENCIL BALANCING

Leo Bircher of Switzerland balanced a pencil upright on his nose for a time of 2 minutes, 33 seconds.

## PEOPLE BALANCING

On 23 July 2000, John Evans of Heanor, Derbyshire, UK, achieved the record for balancing the most people on his head in one hour, with a tally of 92 different people, set at an exhibition held in Lowestoft, UK.

## PIANO THROWING

On 10 March 1983, a team of 6 men from Newcastle University, UK, set a world record for piano throwing of 3.54 m (11 ft 6 ins) during their Community Action Week of fundraising events.

The female record was set by a team of 6 from the University of Birmingham, UK, Wendy Hudson, Ali

Tovey, Samantha Dale, Angela Hobbs, Emmerline Foster and Jane Gibbons, with a throw of 0.91 m (3 feet) on 16 November 1985.

## PIGEON MASS RELEASE
A record number of 170,000 racing pigeons were released on 9 May 1987 at five places in East Berlin (Germany). This was part of the WWII-end anniversary celebrations.

## PIPE SMOKING
The longest period of time a pipe has been smoked by one person without re-lighting is 3 hours, 18 minutes, 15 seconds. Gianfranco Ruscalla (Italy) set this record in 2003. The female record is held by Danuta Pytel (Poland) with a time of 3 hours, 8 minutes, 9 seconds. Competitions must be held under the supervision of the CIPC (Comite International des Pipe Clubs).

## PLAYING CARDS – DECK SORTING
This record requires that the deck of 52 cards must be well shuffled immediately prior to the challenge. It has to be sorted as fast as possible. At the end of the attempt, the sorted deck of cards should be on the table with the backside up.

Stephan Gruber (Germany) set the world record of 45.4 sec on 27 October 2002 in Munich.

## PLAYING CARD THROWING

Lyndhurst, Ohio, USA, resident, Rick Smith Jr, broke the record for throwing a playing card the furthest on 22 March 2002 when he threw a playing card from a fresh deck of cards a distance of 66 m (216 ft 4 in). Rick, a magician since the age of 7, can slice bananas in half and pierce watermelons with the cards thrown from a distance.

## PLAYING CARDS UNDERWATER

Between 28 and 29 September 1991, Peter Liebmann, Robert Menge and Axel Weißbach, of Germany, played cards underwater for 30 hours, 20 minutes using scuba equipment.

## PLAYING LUDO UNDERWATER

Four divers from Hartberg, Austria, played the game of ludo underwater for 41 hours, 40 minutes between 23 and 24 July 1997 in Graz, Austria.

## PLAYING MONOPOLY UNDERWATER
A team of 5 in Alost, Belgium, played Monopoly underwater for 30 hours, 15 minutes between 31 May and 1 June 1997.

## PLOUGHING
Demonstrating an amazing feat of endurance, Edgar Heyl, of Eggenstein, Germany, ploughed for 300 hours, taking a 50-minute rest break after each 10 completed hours. Achieved between 10 and 22 November 1990.

## POGO STICK
The fastest human over 100 m on a pogo stick is Stuart Craven, of Scunthorpe, South Humberside, UK, who recorded 42.85 seconds on 13 July 1986 at Patrington Haven, North Humberside, UK.

## POLE SITTING
Following the strict rules of the 'Pole Sitting World Championships', Daniel Baraniuk of Poland, broke the world record in 2002 when he sat on a 2.5-m (8.2-ft) pole for 196 days in an amusement park in Soltau, Germany. He won against 8 opponents, the first of whom left the contest after just 16 hours of competing.

## POTATO CATCHING

Dean Gould, of Felixstowe, Suffolk, UK, caught 10 potatoes in a bucket thrown one at a time by Mark Hillman over a distance of 30.48 m (100 ft) in the world record time of 37 seconds at a local playing field in March 1987.

## POTATO PEELING

The longest marathon spud bashing ever completed was one lasting 50 hours by Terry Smith, 39, of Hull, Humberside, UK, from 13 to 15 August 1985. During the record-breaking marathon, Terry peeled an incredible 731.2 kg (1,612 lb) of potatoes.

## PUB CRAWLING

The greatest number of British counties visited by way of imbibing at separate hostelries and inns (pub crawling) is 14 – Derbyshire, Warwickshire, Staffordshire, West Midlands, Hereford, Worcestershire, Gloucestershire, Oxfordshire, Buckinghamshire, Bedfordshire, Northamptonshire, Cambridgeshire, Lincolnshire, Leicestershire and Nottinghamshire. The time limit is set at 5½ hours, and motoring speed limits must be adhered to. Ranjit Johal, David Selvey, Patrick Bevan and Peter Gilbert set the record on 21 December 1985.

The longest pub-crawl ever attempted began at 5.35 pm on Friday 18 July 1986 at the Railway Inn, Saltash, Cornwall, UK. From there the team of 5 – Ranjit Johal, Donald Smith, Patrick Bevan, David Selvey and Jacquie Lamb – visited one pub in every mainland county of Great Britain, all 62 of them. The crawl ended 76 hours, 42 minutes later at the Bubble Inn, Stenson, Derbyshire, at 10.17 pm on Monday, 21 July 1986.

However, the ultimate record for visiting as many pubs as possible was reported in New Zealand: it took New Zealander Doug Montgomery 11 years to visit all 1,130 inns listed in New Zealand's telephone directories.

## PUDDING PLONKING

At the 'Alternative Olympics' on 12 June 1988, at the Costello International Sports Stadium, Hull, UK, Peter Dowell set a new pudding plonking record by propelling a 0.7 kg (1.5 lb) black pudding, with the aid of a frying pan, a distance of 36 m (118 ft 2 in).

## QUEUING

The longest recorded time that anyone has ever queued is 4 ½ months. Jeff Tweiten and John Goth of Seattle, Washington, USA, began queuing outside the

Cinerama movie theatre in Seattle to be the first moviegoers waiting to see *Star Wars II: Attack of the Clones*. Arriving at the cinema on 1 January 2002, the duo waited in all weather until the film opened on 16 May 2002.

## RICKSHAW PULLING

Covering a distance of 2,175 km (1,351.5 miles) in 50 days, Sitdek Ahmad Ali of Malaysia hand pulled a rickshaw from 1 October to 19 November 2000, and travelling a distance between 50 km and 80 km (31–50 miles) per day.

## ROLLER COASTER MARATHON

Starting from 23 May 2002, multiple record breaker for marathon roller coaster riding, Richard Rodriguez, 44, a teacher from Chicago, Illinois, USA, spent 104 days on the roller coaster 'Expedition Ge Force' in Haßloch, Germany. According to the rules, he had to ride the coaster non-stop for 10 hours each and every day, however, during the 'summer nights' at Holiday Park, Richard spent 15 hours a day on the ride. The total riding time was 1,112 hours, which equates to 20 circuits every hour, and a total number of 22,240 circuits on 'Expedition Ge Force.'

One year later, Richard set an even more challenging record. From 10 July to 28 August 2003, he rode 'Expedition Ge Force' again, this time almost non-stop – with only a 5 minutes per hour break time allowed. In 49 days he rode 30,000 km (18,642 miles).

## RUBBER BAND BALL

The world's biggest ball of rubber bands was made by John Bain from Wilmington, Delaware (USA). Weighing more than 1250kg (2800 lb), the ball was made from 550,000 rubber bands. The British record belongs to Tony Evans of Portmead, Swansea, Wales. His ball contains six million rubber bands, and took Tony five years to make. in 2003, his ball was dropped from a US Army helicopter in a stunt for American TV Show *Ripley's Believe It or Not*, to see if it would bounce. However, the ball, which weighed 1,189 kg (2,600 lb) did not bounce – it created a massive crater in the earth.

## SCHOOLING MARATHON

A high school class in Görlitz, Germany, broke the record for the longest schooling session ever with a time of 81 hours. The pupils were very disappointed with a teacher who set a written test in one of the last remaining hours.

## SEDAN CHAIR BEARING

In May 1980, six track and field athletes from the sports club Kassel–Wehlheiden, Germany carried a sedan chair weighing 30 kg (66.1 lb) (with a puppet sitting in the chair) non-stop for 25 hours, 5 minutes.

## SHIP PULLING

The heaviest ship ever pulled without the use of vehicles, boats or machinery, was the Stena Germanica, which weighs 23,000 tonnes. On 2 October 2002, the ship was pulled a distance of 20m (65.6 ft) by approximately 1,000 people from Kiel, Germany, for a German television show. The ship is 175 m (547.14 ft) long and 29 m (95.14 ft) high.

## SIGN LANGUAGE

Vicar Michael Sabell set a world record for non-stop 'talking' in sign language, on 2 November 1987 at Sheffield, Yorkshire, UK, of 12 hours exactly. In doing so he raised £400 for the deaf.

## SINGING (NON-STOP)

Eamonn McGirr broke the world record for singing non-stop (using a 5-minute rest per hour permitted) by singing for 10 days, 22 hours. Eamonn, a former club entertainer who had chart success in 1966 with 'Up Went Nelson', first broke the record in 1979 when he sang non-stop for 132 hours, 45 minutes (5½ days)

## SLOWEST LETTER

The letter was received in 1978 by the Chinese trade ministry, and was sent 384 years earlier to the Chinese Emperor, and somehow got lost 'for a while'. The subject of the letter was still a current one as it was suggesting good conditions for foreign salesman in China to support the trade.

## SNAKES

The longest time anyone has spent together in a room with snakes is 100 days. Jürgen Hergert, of Schladen, Germany, spent 100 days in a room that measured 5 m x 6 m (16.4 ft x 19.7 ft) in Gulf Breeze, Florida, USA with 24 poisonous snakes.

## SNOW SCULPTURE

The world's tallest snow sculpture was a 13-m-(42-ft)-tall polar bear, made from 160 tons of snow by four artists at Langjökull (Island).

## SPACE HOPPING

The fastest time to cover 100 m (328.1 ft) on a space hopper is 28.5 seconds by 11-year-old Tony Smythe of Stretchford, Birmingham, UK, at the Birmingham Students Carnival on 16 November 1985.

The greatest height ever cleared on a space hopper is one of 76.2 cm (30 in) by Janina Pulaski on BBC TV on 26 May 1975.

A new space hopper long jump record of 2 m (6 ft 7 in) was set by Vincent Straker, 12, of Peterborough, Cambridgeshire, UK, on 27 May 1990.

## SPIKE BENDING

Georges Christen of Luxemburg bent 368 iron nails (210 mm [8.3 in] long, diameter 7 mm) into a 'U' or 'V' shape within a time of 1 hour.

## SPINNING THE LONGEST THREAD

Terri DeHetre, of New Port Richey, Florida, USA, broke the record for spinning the longest thread of raw wool with a measurement of 671.32 m (734 yd) at the Longest Thread Contest held at the International Highland Spin-In in Bothwell, Tasmania, Australia on 7 March 1997.

## SPOON HANGING

Spoon hanging is the art of balancing the bowl of a spoon on the end of the nose, with the handle hanging down towards the chin. Keeping her head at an angle of 90 degrees to her body and using a standard teaspoon, Ami Barwell, aged seven, of Hedon, North Humberside, UK, 'spoon hung' for 2 hours, 15 minutes, 40 seconds continuously on 10 March 1985.

## STAMPS – LOOSENING FROM LETTERS

French stamp collector Henri Pereira loosened 60,171 stamps from envelopes in the record time of 47 hours, 48 minutes on 2-3 September 1989. It took the philatelist 15 months to collect all the letters in able to set the record.

## STAMP LICKING

In July 2000, Dean Gould, of Felixstowe, Suffolk, UK, set a record for licking and affixing the most postage stamps in 5 minutes. At a local sporting occasion, Dean managed to lick and affix 235 stamps to envelopes at the Brackenbury Sports Centre, Felixstowe.

## STRAWBERRY PICKING
On 2 July 1987 a group of 200 London school children claimed a world record for strawberry picking when they picked 569.7 kg (1,256 lb) of strawberries in 90 minutes.

## TELEPHONE DIRECTORY TEARING
The oldest man to tear up a telephone directory is Léon Christen of Luxembourg, who achieved this on his 94th birthday on 12 January 2001.

## TIDDLYWINKS – FASTEST MILE
This record is for the fastest time to squidge a tiddlywink over a distance of one mile.
*2 players* – 52 minutes, 10 seconds, by Edward Wynn and James Cullingham (both UK) in Stradbroke, Suffolk, UK, on 31 August 2002.
*1 player* – 1 hour, six minutes, 1 second by Ralf Laue (Germany) on 9 November 2003 in Stamberg, Germany.

Both records were achieved on indoor courses.

## TIE KNOTTING
The fastest time ever recorded for knotting a tie is 4.07 seconds. Hans Georg Prinz (Germany) achieved the record with the 'classic' Windsor knot in a contest held in Ingolstadt during 2003.

## TRACTOR PULLING

On 28 March 1998, 3 men from North Carolina, USA, set a world record by pulling a 12,247.2-kg (27,000-lb) tractor-trailer a distance of 1.6km (1 mile) in the record time of 95 minutes, 16 seconds. Kirk Nobles, John Brookfield and Steve Jeck completed the mile-long feat in the presence of Fairmont, North Carolina Mayor Pro Tem, Charles Kemp, who doubled as official timekeeper.

## TRAIN PULLING – WITH TEETH

Georges Christen of Luxemburg pulled a 20.5-ton (20-tonne) railway carriage with his teeth for a distance of 200 m (220 yd) on 18 August 1985.

## TRUCK CARRYING

Arnie Scoles and Dick Reed of the Power Source Health Club, Los Angeles, USA, hold the world record for truck carrying with a time of 55.5 seconds. The pick-up truck must weigh at least 1,301.8 kg (2,870 lb) and the rear wheels must be lifted off the ground. The truck is then carried along a 36.57-m (40-yd) course.

## TRIAL MOTORCYCLE – DRIVING ON BACK OF HANDLEBAR

In Douai, France, Jean-Pierre Goy set the distance record for riding a trial motorcycle while on the back of its handlebars on 7 December 1991 when he covered a distance of 31 km (19.26 miles) in 30 minutes. He also has another record under more difficult circumstances. At night, on an unlit circuit of Motocross and without rear-view mirrors or headlamps, Jean-Pierre travelled a distance of 9.650 km (6 miles) in a time of 30 minutes on 24 July 1993.

## TRUCK PULLING

Olympic shot-putter and former 'World's Strongest Man' Geoff Capes, broke his own world record for solo truck pulling at Dover, Kent, UK, on 18 September 1986. Geoff dragged the 12.5-tonne truck the required distance of 25 m (82 ft) in 42.31 seconds.

## TYPING

Barbara Blackburn of Salem, Oregon, USA, is the fastest typist in the world. Using the Dvorak Simplified Keyboard, rather than the standard 'Qwerty' keyboard, she is able to maintain a speed of 150 wpm for 50 minutes – an amazing 37,500 key strokes. Her fastest speed was recorded at 212 wpm. The key to her success is the keyboard design. Blackburn will type on nothing but the Dvorak keyboard, in preference over the standard 'Qwerty' keyboard, which has vowels on one side and consonants on the other, with the most frequently used letters on the centre row.

## ONE-FINGER TYPING

The fastest one-finger typist is Farhat Khan, of Bhopal, India, who can type 60 words in 1 minute in either Hindi or English using an electronic typewriter.

## TYPING NUMBERS INTO WORDS

On 25 November 1998, after 16 years at the typewriter, Les Stewart, of Mudjimba, Australia, reached his goal of typing every number from one to one million – in words (not numbers) on his manual machine. He started his marathon task in 1982 as therapy following an accident and a serious illness. Seven manual typewriters, 1,000 ink ribbons, 19,890 pages, 16 years and seven months later, he finished with the lines 'nine hundred and ninety-nine thousand, nine hundred and ninety-nine', then 'one million'.

When asked why he undertook this time-consuming and repetitious task, Les says that he had little else to do now that he has been classed as an invalid, and can no longer work. Besides that, Les enjoys typing and used to be a police typing instructor before his sickness which meant his withdrawal from the force. Typing an average of 3 pages a day with one finger since April 1982, Les said his secret was to type for 20 minutes on the hour, every hour.

## TYPED PAINTING

Uday Mahadeo Talwalkar (India) has typed the largest typewritten 'painting' – a portrait of Lata Mangeshkar measuring 6.50 m x 4 m (21.4 ft x 13.3 ft).

## TYPING MARATHON

The marathon record for typing is held by Gisela Ewald (Germany) with a time of 276 hours.

## UNICYCLE – TALLEST

On 29 January 2004, Sem Abrahams, of USA, successfully pedalled a 35-m (115-ft) tall unicycle in his home town of Livonia. Abrahams owns a company called Semcycle together with his former unicycle world champion wife Teresa. Abrahams has set world records previously, at 14 m (45 ft) and 22 m (72 ft) tall. The new cycle stands as tall as his previous two cycles stacked on top of each other.

## WALK AROUND THE WORLD

Friedrich Kustav Kögel (Germany) was the first person reported to have walked around the world in 1896. However, there is no written documentation about his record.

Dave Kunst (USA) is the first man verified to have completed circling the entire landmass of earth (with exception of the oceans) on foot. Between 20 June 1970 and 5 October 1974, Dave walked 23,254.4 km (14,450 miles) around the planet. Starting from the East in Waseca, Minnesota, USA, with his brother John (who was killed by bandits in Afghanistan in 1972), Kunst crossed 4 continents and 13 countries, wearing out 21 pairs of shoes and walking more than 20 million steps. His other brother, Pete, took the place of John, and together they returned to Waseca, Minnesota from the West.

## WALKING ON WATER

There was a time when walking on water was merely a miracle of biblical proportions. As part of a competition to kick off the Edinburgh Science Festival held in Scotland on 11 April 2003, the first 40-m (131.2-ft) water sprinting competition was held. Twenty-one teams competed, and a group of friends calling themselves Gemeni Dawn set the 40-m (131.2-ft) record in a time of 1 minute, 10 seconds. Using very large shoes made mostly of polyurethane, the team also won the category for the fastest shoes built for less than £50.00.

## WASHING CARS
A full-time car washer by profession, Otto Dettl of Austria washed 188 cars in 72 hours, setting a new endurance world record in 1985.

## WATER BAILING
This record is the quickest time taken to bail a 'pond-sized' amount of water out of a single receptacle. The volume is now set at 170 imperial gallons and the bailing record using a No 1. Size thimble is held by 12 children of the Chesterfield Young Oxfam Group, who on 15 March 1975 completed their task in 12 hours exactly.

## WATER-FILLED WELLY WANGING

Always a popular and entertaining feature of holiday camp fun and games, water-filled welly wanging has now become established as a regular World Championship event. Competitors must be seated in a chair or stool and throw the size-10 welly full of water backwards over the head. The distance is measured to the first contact point with the ground.

At the first Annual Water Filled Welly Wanging Championships at The Black Horse Inn, Roos, Humberside, UK, on 25 January 1986, a world record throw of 15.42 m (50.59 ft) was achieved by Mel Brewer, 27, of Bradford, West Yorkshire, UK. At the same event a new female record was set at 7.62 m (25 ft) by Jean Bramhall, 25, of Bradfield, West Yorkshire, UK.

## WEATHER BALLOON INFLATING

The shortest time taken to inflate two 1,000-g (35.3-oz) weather balloons consecutively to 2.5 m (8 ft) diameter using only lung power is 4 hours, 42 minutes, 23 seconds by Fred Burton of Cheadle, Staffordshire, UK, on 13 June 1982.

## WEB PAGE, MOST TRANSLATED

The world's most translated web page is www.rekordfestival.de/english.html, currently translated into 114 different languages, including Glosa, Papiamentu and even Klingon. Translations into more languages are welcome!

## WEDDING VEIL

When Eva Hofbauer (Austria) married in June 2004 in Korneuburg, more than 800 children were left outside the church. They were all needed to support Eva's bridal veil – an incredible 2,812.55 m (9227.53 ft) of it!

## WHEEL CHANGING

The fastest recorded time for changing all four wheels (four stud) on a family saloon car using only manual tools is 2 minutes, 30 seconds by a team of four from Industrial Tyre Specialists, Hull, at Patrington Haven, Humberside, UK, on 13 July 1986.

The individual record is held by Ulrich Haas (Germany) who changed all four wheels on a family saloon car in 5 minutes, 8 seconds.

## WING WALKING

An 88-year-old Second World War hero became the oldest person to stand on the wing of an aeroplane on 20 August 2002. Leslie 'Dizzy' Seales, of Shoreham, Sussex, UK, broke the record, previously held by an 87-year old South African woman, by standing on the wing of a 1940s Boeing Stearman for 10 minutes. However, not satisfied with this, he notched up a further seven flights, flying for a total of three-quarters of an hour.

The oldest woman ever to complete the wing-walking stunt is 80-year-old grandmother of 14 Paddy Hayes. Mrs Hayes, of Bressingham, near Diss, UK, was strapped on to a Boeing Stearman for 8 to 10 minutes, and carried out the challenge at the Clacton Airshow on 22 August 2003 as a charity fundraiser for the Parkinson's Disease Society and the Cinnamon Trust

## WORM CHARMING

At the Annual World Worm Charming Championships held at Willaston School, Nantwich, Cheshire, UK, on 19 July 1980, Tom Shufflebottom set a new world record by successfully charming 511 worms to the surface in the allotted 30 minutes. Entrants are given a plot of land 3 sq m (32.3 sq ft) and are then required to 'insert an ordinary kitchen fork into the soil and vibrate it'.

# THE AMAZING ...
# DEAN GOULD

*'I always wanted to be the best at something...'*
Dean Gould

'Dextrous Dean' is a name that has stuck with Dean Gould since a visit to Hamburg in the 1980s. Born in Ipswich in 1964, Dean exhibited a talent for weird and unusual feats from a young age, harbouring an ambition to be a record breaker as a child, an ambition which was realised in 1984 when he smashed the beer mat flipping record of 67 with a catch of 90 on BBC television's *Record Breakers*. Dean broke this record on several occasions thereafter, and his current best is 111, though the record has recently been beaten.

Since 1984, Dean has gone on to break and set more records in different disciplines than any other living record breaker during his 18-year career, dominating the dextrous and speed record circuit, achieving a status that can assure him a place in the top ten world record breakers of all time.

Dean's record tally currently stands at more than 20, holding records for coin snatching, egg balancing, needle threading, pancake tossing, stamp licking, rice eating, winkle picking and beer mat flipping.

He is thrilled to have achieved so many records. 'It's brilliant – I never thought I would get so many. People will obviously come forward and challenge some of them, that goes without saying,' says Dean.

His talent may be attributed to his amazing hyper-

61

extendible fingers, possessing the ability to turn his fingers outwards so as to cup things on the backs of his hands, a skill he has had since a small boy.

At 39, he knows there are limitations to what he is now capable of doing, but for now there are no signs that the multi-record holder is about to give up or retire. Setting new records for coin snatching and compact disc flipping, we can expect Dean to be appearing on the record-breaking circuit for many more years.

Now living in Felixstowe, he is a local celebrity and father of three. Dean often lends his 'dextrous' hands to charity work, having competed at televised events such as BBC's Children in Need, and more recently BBC's Sport Relief.

## DEAN'S WORLD RECORDS INCLUDE:

### BEER MAT SPEED FLIPPING
Flipping 25 piles of 40 mats on the edge of a table and catching 1,000 in a record time of 45 seconds.

### BEER MAT CATCHING
Dean balanced a stack of 2,400 beer mats on his forearm, then proceeded to catch them falling in the palm of his hand, catching 2,390 beer mats.

## COIN SNATCHING

Dean placed 482 10p coins on his forearm, then
proceeded to snatch them palm down from the air,
catching 328 coins.

Dean placed 100 10p coins on his forearm, then
proceeded to snatch them palm down from the air,
without dropping any.

## EGG BALANCING

Dean balanced 13 size-6 eggs on the back of
one hand.

## STAMP LICKING

Licking and sticking 235 stamps to envelopes in
5 minutes.

## COMPACT DISC FLIPPING

Dean flipped and caught a stack of compact discs
balanced on the edge of a table, 180 degrees and
caught 45.

# THE AMAZING ...
# RALF LAUE

*'I had 28 successful record attempts so far, but I often failed when I try to break my own records – it's not as challenging as beating another competitor...'*
Ralf Laue

Ralf Laue is a rare breed of man, a person who has turned his lifelong hobby into a healthy obsession. Born on 25 April, 1968, Ralf has had an interest in world records since the tender age of 12, collecting information related to world records that has grown into an extensive archive and library, including over 200 books about records from all over the world.

Ralf broke his first world record in 1986, for the largest fan of cards held in one hand. Since then he has broken many records, and has held 16 records during the course of his record-breaking career. He studied mathematics at the University of Leipzig and now works as a computer specialist. He lives in Leipzig, Germany, with his wife Silke and daughter Jana.

In 1988, Ralf's on-going love affair with world records lead him to form the *Rekord-Klub SAXONIA*, an international club for people who have broken unusual records, and then a record-breaking web site (www.recordholders.org).

'I prefer records that can be tried at home without too much preparation,' he begins. 'In the past few years, my favourite subject are records for memory and mental calculation. The most difficult record so far was to solve three Rubik's cubes from memory while blindfolded.'

When asked about the future, Ralf provides an apt response. 'Of course, there are challenges for the future: more records for balancing, speed and memory. I have twenty-eight successful record attempts so far, but I failed often when I tried to break my own records – it's not as challenging as beating another competitor.'

## RALF'S WORLD RECORDS INCLUDE:

### LARGEST FAN OF CARDS
326 cards in one hand, colour and value of each one visible, 18 March 1994, Leipzig, Germany.

### DOMINO STACKING
Domino stacking (555 dominoes on top of a vertical one), 2 July 1999, Cologne, Germany. This record has recently been beaten.

### PANCAKE TOSSING
Flipped a pancake 416 times in 2 minutes, 28 June 1997, Linz, Austria.

### SORTING RUBIK'S CUBES BLINDFOLDED
Sorting 3 Rubik's Cubes while blindfolded, 3 February 2001, Halle, Germany.

# 4

# COLLECTING THE BIGGEST, THE LONGEST AND THE SMALLEST

## ABACUS

Two teachers from the Soroban Education Centre, in Singapore, constructed the world's longest abacus tool. Phyilly Wong and Yen Chiu Jung constructed the abacus on 31 July 1998. The abacus, measuring 4.88 m (16 ft) long and 13 cm (5.11 in) wide, contained 1,200 counting beads on 240 columns, and can be used by up to 18 people at one time.

The world's smallest abacus was made by miniature sculptor Chen Yu Pei, of Shanghai, China. The abacus, measuring 5 mm x 11.5 mm (0.2 in x 0.5 in) has 77 beads, which are arranged in 11 columns of 7 beads each.

## AIRLINE BAGGAGE TAGS

A 14-year-old Indian boy created the world record for the largest collection of airline baggage tags in the world. Raghav Somani, of the southern city Chennai, India, collected 469 tags in the space of 10 years. The collection includes tags made of leather and metal and even includes special tags used for animals, and those issued by Continental Airlines for US Republicans attending a national convention in 1992.

## BABY CHAIR
The biggest baby chair was made by M. Jimenez, and exhibited at the Record Festival in La Tour Blanche, France. It stands 3.03 m (9.94 ft) high.

## BALLPOINT PENS
Angelika Unverhau, of Dinslaken, Germany, has accumulated more than 250,000 different ballpoint pens. On average, she acquires an additional 30,000 new pens each and every year. She founded a club for ballpoint pen collectors, and her favourite pen is a Russian ballpoint pen made in 1957 to celebrate the launch of Sputnik 1.

## BARBECUE GRILL
The world's largest barbecue grill was held in May 2003 during a three-day conference in Dagupan, Philippines. Measuring 1,007.59 m (3,305.7 ft) without gaps, the grill was arranged for a grill party, where it was estimated that 120,000 revellers partied until the early hours of the morning – beating the previous year's attendance by 20,000.

## BARBED WIRE
Anthony J. Spellman, of Phoenix, Arizona, USA, claims to have the world's largest collection of

different types of barbed wire. One of his rooms houses 72 different types.

## BARF BAGS

The largest collection of 'airsickness' bags was amassed by marketing and investment consultant Niek Vermeulen of the Netherlands who has the world's largest collection of 'barf bags' with over 3,728 optical different bags from over 802 different airlines (counted in March 2004) and a further 10,000 spare bags.

Niek and his family embark upon nearly 70 international flights each year, harvesting sickbags along the way. Friends also aid Niek by bringing him any unusual 'barf bag' specimens they come across in their travels. His favourite bag is an airsickness bag from a NASA space shuttle, which spent 16 days in space.

Niek is always interested in contact with other collectors (e-mail: lynternet@hotmail.com).

## BEER TRAY (LARGEST)

The biggest tray for serving beer could carry 1,000 glasses, and measured 27.40 m (89.89 ft) in length. Made by Rainer Drechsler, of Germany, a crane was used for serving the beer and, for the record to be achieved, no beer was spilled. The record was set in 2002 for a German TV show.

## BENCH

Hand crafted by 1,200 volunteers, the world's longest bench was made on 22 November 2003 at a park in Kanuma, Tochigi Prefecture, Japan. The bench measuring 550 m (1,804 ft) was made from local cedar, and made to commemorate the 55th anniversary of the city's becoming a municipality. Organised by Mori no Nakama, a group of wood craftsman, the Kanuma bench was assembled on a cherry-tree-lined embankment in Deai no Mori Sogo Koen Park. Participants nailed wooden legs to a seat board and a back panel to make 367 benches, each 1.5 m (4.90 ft) long. These were then fastened together using plates and screws.

## BICYCLE

Built by Didi Senft, of Kolpin, Germany, the biggest scaled-up bicycle in the world is 7.80 m (25.59 ft) long and 3.7 m (12.14 ft) tall. Didi can ride this bicycle, though wears a crash helmet for safety due to the increased risks of an accident. Didi has built more than 100 unusual bicycles, and holds other vehicle records including the biggest rickshaw, which is 12.38 m (40.62 ft) long.

The tallest cycle was built by Brad Graham of Thunder Bay, Ontario, Canada. His two-wheeled bicycle measures 5.49 m (18 ft) tall which he rode for 300 m (984.3 ft), beating his own record for the 4.43-m-tall (14 ft 3 in) 'SkyCycle'.

## BIRD MUNCHIE

During 1998, as part of an exhibition in the highly successful Sydney Pet and Animal Expo, Vortex Industries Property Ltd decided that they needed something eye catching to get people's attention. Somebody suggested a 'giant bird munchie' as a joke. Three weeks later, the bird munchie had been made weighing 650 kg (1,430 lb). Although it started out as a joke, the exhibit was well received, so much so that it was taken to Brisbane a few months later for the 2nd Brisbane Pet and Animal Expo. After the shows, the world's biggest bird munchie was taken to a local park in Canberra where wild birds feasted on all 650 kg (1,430 lb) of the extra large treat.

## BLANKET

Devon pensioner Val Stone spent 11 years crocheting the world's largest blanket. Starting in 1988, just before she was diagnosed with leukaemia, Mrs Stone fashioned the blanket herself stating that no square of the blanket is alike. Measuring 24 m (78 ft) by 8 m (27 ft) when stretched out, it weighs 90 kg (198 lb). In September 2001, parts of the blanket were sold to raise money for the Exeter Leukaemia Fund, and the remainder was to be sold at later events to raise upwards of £3,000 for the worthy cause.

## BOOK

The smallest book, with a print run of more than 1,000 copies is Joshua Reichart's *ABC Picture Book*. It measures only 2.4mm x 2.9mm. The miniature book was published in Leipzig, Germany in 2000. It has 32 pages.

## BOOT

The biggest boot in the world was made with leather from ten cows, and put together by a team from Döbeln, Germany, under the leadership of Rolf Neidhardt of Leisnig, Germany. The boot measured 4.90 m (16.07 ft) tall and 2.20 m (7.217 ft) long, weighing 439 kg (967.8 lb). After taking 1,100 working hours, the boot was completed and presented in 1996.

## BOTTLE TOPS

The largest collection of bottle tops belongs to Günter Offermann, of Hamburg, Germany. He has collected 103,000 beer bottle tops from 177 different countries.

## BOUNCY BALLS

As of July 2002, the biggest collection of bouncy-balls in the world so far is 1,300. Collected by Chris Decker, 18, of Milford, Connecticut, USA, he started collecting the super-high bouncing balls in March 2001.

## CARPET

The record for the longest carpet in the world was reportedly broken twice during the summer of 2003. A red carpet was made in Passau, Germany, measuring 2 km (1.2 miles) in length. The record was further beaten on 6 September 2003, when an even longer carpet was created in Schweich, Germany, measuring 2.7 km (1.6 miles) in length. However, what the German record breakers did not know was the record had already been broken in Oman. The Sultan of Oman ordered the longest of all 'longest red carpets'. Made by Dattajirao Kadam Textile Institute in Ichalkaranji, India, the carpet stretched between palaces of the sultan – a staggering 4 km (2.50 miles) long.

## CATWALK

The world's longest catwalk was constructed in the car park of the Seacon Square shopping complex on the outskirts of Bangkok, Thailand in 1998. The catwalk covers 14,769 sq m (158,972 sq ft) and is 1,111 m (3,645 ft) long beating the previous world record set in Germany of 1,001 m (3,284 ft). Between 27 and 30 May 1988, more than 100 models paraded on the catwalk, however only one group of 11 models walked the catwalk's entire length.

## CHAIR

The biggest chair in the world was built by Oliver Bierhoff of Germany (not the footballer!), in Udine, Italy. The chair weighed 910 kg (2,006 lb), and stood 20 m (65 ft) tall.

## CHAMBER POTS

Manfred Klauda, of Munich, owns the world's largest collection of chamber pots with more than 9,400. Some of them are shown in his 'Centre of Unusual Museums'.

## CHEESE LABELS

Some people collect stamps, others coins, however Heinz Boltshauser of Switzerland collects cheese labels. Heinz has amassed the world's largest collection with a tally of 165,155 labels from 78 different countries (counted in 2003).

## CHRISTMAS TREE

On 20 December 1999, a towering Eucalyptus regnans in Tasmania was measured to be the tallest ever Christmas tree in the world. At 80 m (262 ft) tall, a team of climbers spent 8 days decorating the tree, transformed by the inclusion of 3,000 Christmas lights, turning it into a powerful beacon of hope for Tasmania's threatened forests.

## CIGAR LIGHTER

The smallest cigar lighter was assembled by Rolf Jarschel of Germany. Its dimensions are 8.23 mm x 8.75 mm (0.32 in x 0.34 in)

## CIGAR

The world's largest cigar was made by José Castelar Cairo (Cuba) in 2000, using tobacco leafs donated by Alejandro Robaina, considered the best grower in Cuba. It is 11.04 m (36.22 ft) in length.

## COINS

In Sweden, in 1644, due to a lack of silver, plates from copper weighing 15 kg (33 lb), were used as 'coins', thus being the biggest coins ever. It was reported that the ceilings in the houses of rich people often collapsed beneath the weight of these coins.

The world's smallest coins were used in the 13th century in Tartu, Estonia. These coins only weighed 0.12 g (4.23 oz).

## COIN MURAL

On Tuesday, 4 December 2001 the world record for the largest coin mural was set, consisting of an amazing 1,659,000 coins, and depicting a giant Irish coin. The Irish harp as it appears on all Irish coinage is the main feature, and includes the dates '995–2001'. Constructed at the National Museum, Collins' Barracks, Ireland, by members of Foróige, a National Youth Development Organisation, in aid of Pfizer Operation Rudolph that supports many charities across Ireland. The former world record of 1 million coins was set in Minnesota, USA, in 1998 with a mural of Abraham Lincoln.

## CORK

The biggest cork for a bottle was made by the association of the Record Festival in La Tour Blanche, France. The cork stands 3 m (9.8 ft) tall, and weighs 600 kg (1,323 lb). Unfortunately, no scaled-up bottle exists for the cork to be used.

## CROSSWORD PUZZLE

The largest crossword ever to be actually published was by HERBKO International in 1998 under the title 'The World's Largest Crossword Puzzle'. It had 28,000 clues, and over 91,000 squares. The crossword hangs on a full 2 m x 2 m (7ft x 7ft) of wall space, and can take up to a year to complete.

## DANCE FLOOR

The Tavern public bar in Stoneclough near Bolton, UK, is home of the world's smallest dance floor. Measuring just 3 sq m (32 sq ft), the dance floor is just big enough for one person to dance in comfort. The couple who run the pub, Carl Burgess and Nicola Kenny, came up with the idea for a laugh to save re-carpeting costs when they had a pillar removed leaving a bare space in the room.

## DIGGER

The world's tiniest mechanical digger, created by the Institute for Microtechnology, Mainz, Germany, has a total length of 63 mm (6.4 in), and a weight of just 12 g (0.4 oz).

## DOMINOES

Scott Suko, with help from the local Jaycees (an organisation for young people that promotes leadership and business skills), organised the world's biggest game of dominoes. This game, played at the Baltimore, Maryland, Armoury in 1989, used 2.43-m-tall (8-ft-tall) dominoes. These dominoes were so large that four people were required to lift each one.

## EASTER EGGS

The record for the largest collection of Easter eggs is held by the late Eduard Polak, of Vienna, who prior to his death had amassed an amazing collection of 16,200 Easter eggs, including ones from glass, wool, metal and silk, as well as the traditional ones of chocolate.

## ENGINE

The smallest two-stroke engine was built by Ing. Detlef Abraham, of Germany. The engine's measurements are 37 mm x 28 mm x 44 mm (1.5 in x 1.1 in x 1.7 in). The stroke volume is 122 $mm^3$ (7.4 $in^3$).

## FAX
The longest fax ever sent was at the computer fair CeBIT 1993 in Hanover, Germany. The entire Bible was sent to a fax machine at the Toshiba Computer exhibition stand, taking a total of 144 hours, and measuring 2,718.9 m (8,920 ft) in length.

## FLY FOR FLY-FISHING
The biggest handmade fly for fly-fishing was made in 1990 by Andreas Esslinger of Switzerland in 30 working hours. The fly, on completion, weighed 40 kg (88.1 lb) and was 2.56 m (8.39 ft) tall.

## FORK LIFT TRUCK
The tiniest, fully operational fork lift truck in the world has a length of just 23 mm (0.9 in)  and was manufactured by the Institute for Microtechnology, Mainz, Germany.

## GLASS CERAMIC COOKTOP
The largest glass ceramic cooktop ever to be made was manufactured by Schott Glas, Mainz, Germany.

At 3.20 m x 1.20 m (10.4 ft x 3.93 ft), it is 14 times bigger than a standard cooktop and it has more than 40 cooking zones. Needing as much electricity to power as a detached house (65 kW), the appliance was unveiled on 17 April 2002. German celebrity chef Frank Buchholz cooked for guests using the record-breaking piece of glass ceramic.

## GLASS VASE

On 18 August 2003, the world's largest glass vase was made by the company Schott in Zwiesel (Germany). Ten glass artists from Poland worked on the piece, which on completion measured 3.69 m (12.10 ft) in height.

## GLOBE

At 12.5 m (41ft 1½ m) EARTHA, a rotating globe housed in a three-storey atrium at the headquarters of DeLorme (a top mapping publisher) in Yarmouth, Maine, USA, is the world's largest rotating globe. Unveiled on 23 July 1998, it beat the previous record holder, the Globe of Peace in Apecci, Pesaro, Italy, which measured 10 m (33 ft) in diameter – and which was not revolving. Taking two years to build, EARTHA represents Earth as it is seen from space, using a scale of 1:1,000,000, which works out to be

2.54 cm equalling nearly 16 miles (26 km). 'The building of EARTHA was a tremendous challenge for all of us,' says David DeLorme, CEO. 'It will help us make even better maps and will help others envision how we on earth are all connected.'

The 1964 New York World's Fair Unisphere in Flushing Meadows, USA, is 35.57 m (120 ft) in diameter, but it does not rotate.

## THE SMALLEST GLOBE

The world's smallest globe measures 5.3 mm (0.2 in) in height, and the moveable part is 2.99 mm (0.1 in) in diameter. Made by miniature sculptor Chen Yu Pei, of Shanghai, China, the globe was carved on a piece of ivory and then coloured. It took several hundred hours to make during 1987.

## HARP

The world's largest playable harp is the resultant work of Wave Roard Barron, Kristin Novaswan and Lee Barron. Built in 1982 in Santa Fe, New Mexico, United States, it stands 4 m (13 ft 4 in) high, measures 2.25 m (7ft 6 in) in width and 121.9 cm (48 in) in depth, built to a scale of 2½ times as large as a concert harp. The giant harp has an enclosed sound box, a harmonic curve, 41 stainless steel aircraft cable strings, brushed steel revolving base, hand-moulded redwood trunk seat for two, and can be plucked by hand or played by wood.

## HELICOPTER

The smallest flying helicopter in the world has an actual size of just 24 mm (0.9 in) Its height, including rotors is 8 mm (0.3 in), its width 2 mm (0.08 in) and its weight is 400 mg (1.4 oz). It was manufactured by the Institute for Microtechnology, Mainz, Germany.

## HOCKEY STICK

The people of Duncan, Vancouver Island, Canada, are the proud owners of the world's largest ice hockey stick. Commissioned and paid for by the Canadian government at an undisclosed cost for Expo 86 in Vancouver, the stick was shipped from Vancouver to Duncan by barge after the Expo 86 event. On its arrival, the people of Duncan brought out sandpaper and sanded it before hooking it up to a crane and watching as it was raised to the top of the Community Centre. The hockey stick weighs 31 tons, and is 62.5 m (205 ft) long. With its black, brown, white and red colours, it can be seen at night due to the small lights that cover its outside edges.

## HORSESHOES IN A HEN'S EGG

Lajos Kuris, of Hungary, achieved the most horseshoes in a hen's egg. Using 768 nails and 1,536 holes, Mr Kuris managed to fit 192 horseshoes in the egg.

## HOT AIR BALLOON

Gerriet Müller, of Germany, built the smallest model hot air balloon in the world. With a height of 205 mm (8.1 in), and a weight of 3.5 g (0.12 oz), the model balloon flew a height of 9 m (30 ft) for 57 seconds on 20 May 1995.

## KITCHEN TIMERS

The largest collection of kitchen timers belongs to Edeltraut Dreier, of Berlin, Germany. He has amassed a collection of more than 980 different working kitchen timers.

## KITE

Peter Lynn of New Zealand holds the record for the world's largest kite. 'MegaBite' (built in 1995) and 'Mega-Ray' (built in 1997) have both a total lifting area of 635 m² (6,835 ft²), and were both designed by Peter Lynn. 'Mega-Ray' has a 42-m (138-ft) wing span with a body length of 28 m (92 ft). The tail length is 40 m (131 ft 3 in), though the tail is not used for calculating the area of the kite. Both kites were successfully flown on different occasions.

## KNITTED SCARF

The world's longest scarf knitted by a single person is 1,074 m (3,523 ft) long. Ray Ettinger, of Independence, Missouri, USA, began knitting the 18-cm-wide (7-inch-wide) royal blue scarf in 1995, and worked on the woollen garment for five years, using 158 skeins of yarn, to finish in October 2000. At 34 kg (75 lb), the scarf was seven times larger than the previous record of 174 m (571 ft) belonging to an English woman.

## LEGO CAR

Built in Chicago, and using more than 650,000 LEGO components, the LEGO Group's designers worked for 1,500 hours to design a life-size LEGO Super Car, and the company's model builders and technicians spent a further 4,000 hours assembling it. Though the life-size version of the LEGO car is 10 times bigger than the set sold in stores world-wide, it uses 500 times more LEGO elements. The LEGO Super Car is approximately 4.72 m (15 ft 5 in) long, 2.28 m (7 ft 5 in) wide and 1.24 m (4 ft 10 in high), weighing more than a ton, making it the biggest LEGO car in the world.

## LOCK

During 2003 Haji Javed Iqbal Khokhar, of Gujranwala, Pakistan, broke the record for the biggest lock in the world. The lock uses a digital electronic system, has a height of 3.505 m (11 ft 6 in), a width of 1.37 m (4 ft 6 in) and a depth of 63.5 cm (25 in) and weighs a colossal 1,883 kg (4,151 lb), plus a key weight of 120 kg (264½ lb).

The biggest lock that is actually in use was made by Trusty Lock in India. Its height is 2 feet (50 cm) and it weighs about 50 kg (110 lb). It is used in the Jagannath Temple in Orissa. Trusty Lock has also made the smallest handmade lock. Made with silver, it weighs 1.5 g (5.29 oz) and its size is just 4.5 mm (0.18 in).

## LOGO

The biggest logo presented by Quelle in Leipzig, Germany was the size of four football fields, measuring 274 m x 91 m (898 ft x 298 ft 6 in). It took 3 weeks of work using a blue carpet weighing 9,100 kg (20,062 lb) and 1.5 tonnes of small pebbles.

## MIKADO

The biggest game of Mikado was made by Rainer Drechsler, of Germany, and presented at the Rekord-Klub Saxonia Record Festival in Dessau on 29 September 2001. The Mikado sticks were made from wood, and had a length of 5.10 m (17 ft).

## MOUSETRAP

The largest mousetrap ever made measures 4.20 m x 2.07 m (13.77 ft x 6.79 ft), and was created by multi-record breaker Gerd Junghans of Germany.

## NAIL

The world's longest nail has a length of 7 m (22.9 ft). It was made by Manfred and Gert Nagel, of Bad Berka, Germany. Their name 'Nagel' translated means 'nail'.

## NEWSPAPER

Dolores Schwindt, a Brazilian publisher, achieved her family's 75-year-old dream in 2000 when she produced a 16-page monthly newspaper, called *Vossa Senhoria*, measuring just 2.54 cm x 3.56 cm (1 in x 1.4 in) – the world's smallest newspaper. Costing 30p, *Vossa Senhoria* is available throughout Brazil, with a circulation of 5,000. Dolores who lives in

Divinopolis, 532 miles east of Brasilia, also produces another minuscule publication, a paper measuring 4.83 cm x 6.60 cm (1.9 in x 2.6 in). Vossa Senhoria was created in 1935 by the printing worker and self-teaching journalist Leônidas Schwindt, who saw the small size as a solution for creating a quality low-cost newspaper.

## NUT CRACKER

The world's largest collection of nut crackers was amassed by Uwe and Jürgen Löschner, of Neuhausen, Germany. Father and son have collected 4,334 different nut crackers which are displayed in their museum.

The world's largest nut cracker was constructed by Jürgen Löschner as well. It stands 5.87 m (6 yd 1 ft 3 in) tall. The giant nut cracker was made from wood and is able to crack even coconuts.

## PAPER CRANE

The magazine *British Origami* reported that Assistant Professor Watanaba at Nigata University, Japan, used a square measuring 1 mm x 1 mm to fold the smallest paper crane. He used a microscope and sewing needle for his records.

## PAPER FROG

In April 1994, a leap of 74.7 cm (29.4 in) was achieved by an origami frog folded out of photocopy paper measuring 15 cm x 15 cm.

## PEDAL CARS

Manfred Klauda, of Munich, Germany, has collected more than 450 pedal cars, most of them historical models. As well as his record-breaking collection of chamber pots, the most interesting items of his collection can be found at the 'Centre of Unusual Museums' in Munich.

## PENCILS

K. Kasatkin, a journalist from Kiev, Ukraine, has collected more than 5,000 different pencils.

## PERIODIC TABLE

Almost 100 students who attended Varina High School, Richmond, Virginia, USA, took part in creating the world's biggest periodic table. Reminiscent of something you would come to expect to see in a chemistry classroom, the giant table was put together by Varina High School teacher Magaret Godsey and her students. Listing all the recognised elements from hydrogen all the way to number 110, each element had its own poster-size piece of mat board. The pieces were all threaded together with steel cable, then suspended by steel rope on one wall of a rotunda. Measured at 7 m (24 ft) tall and 18.25 m (60 ft) wide, this periodic table is recognised as the largest one in the world.

## PIANO – PLAYABLE
Built by Hubert Molard, of Straßbourg, France, the smallest piano in the world is 25.6 cm (10 in) tall and 15.4 cm (6 in) long. It took 1,500 working hours to make, and can be played with the use of a toothpick.

## PIANO MODEL – NOT PLAYABLE
The smallest model of a piano can be viewed in the museum of miniature instruments by Udo Thein, of Essen, Germany. His smallest item is a piano measuring 2.8 cm (1.1 in) long, 7.7 cm (3 in) high and 6.8 cm (2.67 in) wide.

## PIGGY BANK
The Royal Canadian Mint became a world record holder on 1 July 2004 when it unveiled the world's largest piggy bank at its historic Ottawa headquarters. The piggy bank stands over 4 m (13 ft) tall and measures more than 5.5 m (18 ft) in length.

All funds collected in the world's largest piggy bank will be donated to the Government of Canada Workplace Charitable Campaign. The piggy bank was built as an added attraction for the Royal Canadian Mint Canada Day activities, where visitors have the opportunity to tour the facility and learn about the Mint's 96-year history.

## PLASTIC BOTTLE CHAIN

In August 2002, after taking 10 months, students from the Jurong Institute in Singapore managed to drink and collect 65,000 soft drinks bottles in aid of setting a new world record. After a hole was punched at the base of each bottle, student Calvin Yeo Yew Lim used a fishing line to string the bottles together to make the world's biggest plastic bottle chain. Measured at 13.15 km (8.17 miles), the chain took three hours, 20 minutes to put together. The bottles have been sent to a recycling company, and the money made from the project was put towards the school's Needy Students fund.

## POP-UP BOOK

Designed and built by Roger Culbertson of Lake Worth, Florida, USA, and illustrated by *New Yorker magazine* illustrator Peter de Sève, the world's largest pop-up book is a 75 cm x 1.25 m (2 ft 6 in x 4 ft) version of Aesop's Fables, featuring a 1 m (3 ft 6 in) board donkey that is as large as a real-life German Shepherd dog. The 12-page project began in December 2001 as a challenge by the Cornell Museum of Art and History in Delray Beach, Florida, where Culbertson was preparing a pop-up book exhibition, and was completed in January 2002.

## PYRAMID FROM BOTTLES

The largest pyramid built from glass bottles was completed by 4 people from Eilat (Israel) on 24 November 2003. Taking 30 hours to build, and using 6,000 whiskey bottles, the construction weighed 5 tonnes and measured 6.60 m (21.65 ft) high.

## RAKE

The world's biggest rake has a length of 7 m (23 ft), with a width of 2.33 m (7 ft 6 in). This extra-sized tool was created by Gerd Junghans of Germany.

## RATTLE

Gerd Junghans of Germany holds many records for making large items, including the world's largest rattle, which measures 2.58 m (8.46 ft) in length and 3.04 m (9.97 ft) in height.

## REFRIGERATOR MAGNETS

The world's greatest collector of refrigerator magnets is Louise J. Greenfarb, of Henderson, Nevada (USA). As of February 2002, Greenfarb had accumulated more than 29,000 magnets and by now that number may well be beyond 30,000. The suburban Las Vegas woman has described the collecting as a lifelong passion.

## ROULETTE

The biggest game of roulette was built in August 1990 by the casino Bad Dürkheim, Germany. The roulette wheel had a diameter of 5.67 m (18.6 ft) and was 1.18 m (3.97 ft) tall. The board measured 47 m x 17 m (154.19 ft x 55.79 ft), and each of the 37 number fields was 2.25 m (7.38 ft) long and 1.50 m (4.92 ft) wide. The roulette ball had a diameter of 11 cm (4.33 in), and the diameter of the jettons varied from 38 cm (14.96 in) up to 58 cm (22.83 in).

## RUBBER DUCKS

The largest collection of rubber ducks belongs to Charlotte Lee, of USA, and her husband Marcel who started collecting rubber ducks in 1996. Since then, Charlotte has amassed a collection of more than

1,439 ducks. A truly dedicated collector, the Lees run a rubber duck web site at www.duckplanet.com.

## SAFETY PIN

The world's largest safety pin was made by Zdeněk Hunak, of Pelhřiov, Czech Republic. It is 6.7 m (21.98 ft) long and weighs 45 kg (99.21 lb).

## SATCHEL

In June 2003, a new record for the largest school satchel was achieved. A leather company in Bangalore, India, has manufactured a giant school bag to promote the spirit of education. Made of nylon and spacious enough to accommodate 30 human beings, the 7.62-m-tall (25-ft-tall) bag weighs 65 kg (143 lb), and used 116 m (381 ft) of nylon fabric, with 22 participants taking around one month to make it. With a 5-m (16-ft) handle and a 28-m-long (92-ft-long) zip, the mammoth bag is a huge hit with curious onlookers who are dwarfed by its size.

## SCARECROWS

Residents of Meaford, Southern Ontario, Canada, spent more than a week in October 2002 to put together the world's largest collection of scarecrows. Almost every other home in Meaford had a scarecrow, and the total number counted was 2,041 – almost doubling the previous record that had been set in Portugal in 1998.

## SCISSORS

The smallest working pair of scissors was made of stainless steel by Chen Yu Pei (China) during 2003. Measuring 1.75 mm (0.068 in) long and 1.38 mm (0.054 in) wide – the scissors were just one-quarter the size of the previous record.

## SCYTHE

Made by farmers from Back, Austria, in 1999, the biggest scythe ever made measured 6.64 m (27.78 ft) in length. They also made a pitchfork that measured 8.60 m (28.21 ft), however, the record for this was already held in Pépinster, Belgium, for a fork measuring 20.5 m (67.25 ft) made in 1986.

## SHIP IN A BOTTLE

Johnny H. Reinert, of Herne, Germany, built the biggest ship in a bottle. The model of the ship Lagoda is 68.2 cm (27 in) long, 43 cm (17 in) tall and 11 cm (4.3 in) wide. The bottle containing 129 L (4362 fl oz) had to be made especially for the world record.

## SHOE

Using 74.3 sq m (800 sq ft) of leather, taken from the hides of at least 30 cows, a team of 10 from Marikina, Philippines, undertook the task of beating the world's largest shoe. Commissioned by the City Council, the shoe required 50 pails of glue to paste the sole to the upper part, and special needles to sew the parts together. On completion in 2002, the shoe measured 5.5 m (18 ft) in length, breaking the previous record by nearly 2 m (6 ft 6 in). See also 'Boot'.

## SIGNPOSTS

The largest collection of signposts on display is the Waston Lake, Yukon, signpost forest in Yukon Territory, Canada. Started in 1942 by homesick US Army G.I., Carl K. Lindley of Danville, Illinois, USA, while working on the Alaska Highway, he erected a sign pointing the way, and stating the mileage to his hometown. Other people followed his lead, and are still doing so today. Now signposts number more than 20,000.

## SILK FLOWER

A giant silk flower was manufactured in Sebnitz, Germany, in 1997. The rose is 3.70 m tall and weighs 10 kg (22 lb). The diameter of the bloom is 1.50 m (4.9 ft), and 40 m (131.2 ft) fleece, 50 m (164 ft) silk and 4.5 kg (9.9 lb) wire were used to construct the flower.

One year later, the same crew presented the world's biggest silk flower carpet, made from 3,000 silk flowers over 150 sq m (1614.6 sq ft).

## SILVER FOIL BALL

Canadian non-smoker Edward Atwood, 67, spent three years rolling silver foil from cigarette packets into the world's biggest silver foil ball, weighing 18.5 kg (41 lb) with a circumference of 91 cm (3 ft). Atwood began collecting cigarette packet foils as a hobby while in hospital recovering from a heart attack.

## SLIDE RULE

In 2001, Texas natives Skip Solberg, 51, of Arlington, USA, and Jay Francis, 53, of Richardson, USA, set about beating the 20-year largest slide rule record. Being in engineering and a person who collects slide rules – he has 800 of them – Solberg teamed up with communications engineer Jay Francis, who has amassed a similarly large collection of slide rules (600). On 28 February 2001 in the Lockeed-Martin Aircraft Assembly facility at Air Force Plant 4 in Fort Worth,

Texas, the slide rule named 'The Texas Magnum 1' was unveiled. Measuring 106.85 m (350 ft 6.6 in), and weighing 136 kg (300 lb), the working device takes three men to slide it, and the mathematical tool can calculate to six significant digits.

## SNOWMAN

The largest snowman in the world was made in Bethel, Maine, USA, on 17 February 1999. It was 35.5 m (113 ft 7.5 in) high, and called 'Angus' after Bethel's town mayor, Angus King. Visitors came from all around to view the giant snowman, which melted on 10 June 1999.

A year after the world's largest snowman was made, the residents of Bethel, Maine, USA, set out to make the largest number of snowmen to commemorate the building of Angus. To celebrate, their aim was to have at least 2,000 snowmen built, charging a $2 registration fee for entry. On 19 February 2000, photographs of the 2,000 snowmen were displayed at the Bethel Inn and Country Club.

## SOAP

After starting a fundraiser for the disease Scleroderma after her mother died, Arlington Melissa Johnson and a group of Laneville volunteers spent almost a year collecting the ingredients for the world's largest bar of soap. On 15 March 2003, the bar of soap, complete with scent, was unveiled weighing in at 7,650 kg (16,900 lb) at an organised event called Tons of Suds for Scleroderma. The bar of soap was cut into 70,000 bars and distributed to charities across the world.

## SPINNING WHEEL

The world's smallest spinning wheel was made by Peter Both, of Rostock, Germany from matchsticks. It stands 3.65 cm (1⁷⁄₁₆ in) tall; the wheel–diameter is 1.2 cm (0.47 in).

On the other hand, the biggest spinning wheel is one weighing 155 kg which was made by Max Edlinger, of Austria, within two months. It is 3.70 m (12.1 ft) tall and 1.50 m (4.92 ft) wide. The diameter of the wheel is 2.25 m (7.38 ft).

## SPRING

The largest spring in the world was completed on 6 May 1987 by Ratcliffe Springs Ltd. of West Bromwich, UK. The dimensions were 110 m (360 ft) long, outside diameter 38 mm (1.49 in) and the wire was 6.55 mm (0.26 in) thick. It was used in grain-processing machinery.

**STEAM SHIP**

In 1993, Gerriet Müller, of Germany, built the smallest model steam ship at 103 mm (4.1 in) in length, with a weight of just 38 g (1.34 oz).

**SUGAR**

Marianne Dumjahn of Germany owns the largest collection of sugar bags and packed sugar cubes with more than 303,000 different ones.

**SWORD**

The biggest sword made measured 4.86 m (15.94 ft) in length and weighed 192 kg (423 lb). Forged by Walter Gerber, of Bärau, Switzerland, it took 1,500 working hours to complete.

**TANDEM**

Built by Winfried Ruloffs and Otto Troppmann of Germany, the smallest rideable tandem bike was just 22 cm (8.66 in) long.

**TEA BAG LABELS**

Felix Rotter, of Cologne, Germany, is the proud owner of the world's largest collection of tea bag labels. In 20 years, he has collected more than 10,600 different ones. His collection includes wooden tea bag labels from Latvia and an XXL-sized tea bag with enough tea to brew 8 L (270.5 fl oz).

## TEAPOT

The world's smallest china teapot was made by miniature sculptor Chen Yu Pei, of Shanghai, China. Measuring 4 mm (0.2 in) in height (including the lid) and 6.8 mm (0.3 in) wide (including handle and spout), the teapot can be filled with 0.03 ml water which can be poured through the spout. The diminutive china piece took the best part of half a year to make, and was completed in 1999.

## THERMOMETER

Richard Porter, of Cape Cod, Massachusetts, holds the record for the largest collection of thermometers in the world. Since retiring, the former high school teacher said, 'Someone once told me, if you don't collect something when you retire, you'll end up just collecting dust or moss. So I collect thermometers.' So far, he has accumulated more than 4000 thermometers, which he displays at his thermometer museum at Wareham cottage.

## TOOTHPASTE

Two people share this category for the largest
collection of tubes of toothpaste. They are owned by
Carsten Gutzeit, of Germany, and Val Kolpakov,
owner of Denture Care Clinic, Davenport, USA,
and originally from Russia. Both have collected
more than 1,000 tubes of toothpaste, from 60
different countries. Carsten Gutzeit started his
collection in 1989, and only began because he liked
the design of a toothpaste tube from Israel. Val
Kolpakov has amassed a selection of more exotic
flavours, including extra dry champagne, amaretto
and whiskey.

## TRAFFIC CONES

David Morgan, of Fulbrook, Oxfordshire, UK, owns
the largest collection of traffic cones in the world. In
his possession are more than 500 cones, varying from
137 different designs. But it's a bit of a busman's
holiday, for David has been making traffic cones
since 1961, and on average makes more than one
million cones a year.

## TUNING FORK

The world's biggest tuning fork was made in
December 2000 by Arno Barthelmes of Zella-

Mehlis, Germany. Measuring 1.65 m (5.41 ft) tall the tuning fork weighs 35.5 kg (78.26 lb). Arno's company has produced tuning forks since 1884.

## VENTILATOR
Haji Javed Iqbal Khokhar (Pakistan) made the world's biggest ventilator which stands (13.70 m [45 ft] tall). Each of the three wings measures 12.5 ft (3.8 m), the complete fan weights 3,700 kg (8157 lb).

## WEATHERVANE – TRADITIONAL
The world's largest traditional weathervane is 14.5 m (48 ft) tall, 4.25 m (14 ft) long and weighs 1,950 kg (4,300 lb). The hand-formed aluminium weathervane has a ship on the top, in homage to a Great Lakes lumber schooner named *Ella Ellenwood*, whose homeport was White Lake, off Lake Michigan, Montague, USA.

## WEATHERVANE – UNUSUAL
In Whitehorse, Yukon Territory, Canada, the world's largest and most unusual weathervane is on display at Whitehorse Airport. The DC-3 aeroplane once used by the U.S.A.A.F flying transport missing between India and China is now used as a weathervane. Built in 1942 by Douglas, it was sold after the war to

Canadian Pacific Airlines. Pivoting on its mount, the aircraft always faces the wind.

## WHISKY BOTTLE

The world's largest bottle of whisky was completed on 3 July 1987 when the 1.83-m-tall (6-ft-tall) monster was filled with 185 l (6255.6 fl oz) of Grant's Finest Scotch Whisky at the Glenfiddich Distillery, Dufftown, Banffshire, UK.

## WINE BOTTLE

Wine collectors and connoisseurs can enjoy the world's most prestigious wines in Los Angeles by purchasing the world's smallest bottles of wine. Produced by Klein's Designs of Encino, California, USA, the bottles stand just 1¾ in tall and are replicas of the full-size brethren. Each bottle is hand filled with fine wine, then corked, sealed and labelled authentically, including the correct volume indication of .75cl.

## YARDSTICKS

Ing. Arnulf Bietsch, of Bolsterlang, Germany, has collected more than 30,000 different yardsticks. These he stores in a special room with air conditioning.

## YO-YO

Made by master jeweller Sidney Mobell in 1989, the world's most expensive yo-yo cost $10,000. The Tom Kuhn Mandala Yo-Yo has a logo that is plated in 24 carat gold, and mounted into the sides are 119 gemstones, including 44 diamonds, 25 rubies, 25 emeralds and 25 sapphires.

# THE AMAZING ...
# JOHN EVANS

*'It was always my dream to be in the record books and I have always admired all the people who are ...'*
John Evans

John Evans has a good head for ideas. You could say that his life has always been a 'balancing' act.

The 56-year-old from Heanor, Derbyshire, UK, is a phenomenon. A grizzled veteran of the world record breaking circuit.

The retired builder has a strange hobby, one that requires the carrying of anything and everything on his head. A phone box, a mini cooper, 10 beer barrels, a 14-ft canoe with a bikini-clad girl in it, 101 house bricks, a coffin. And one Christmas, even a tree will all the trimmings! You name it and John has tottered beneath it.

Although he didn't realise it at the time, John began his hobby when he was 18, while working as a brickie's labourer. 'I started to carry the bricks on my head when I went up ladders,' he explains. 'I could carry twice as many bricks as anyone else, and before long I was carrying up to 24 bricks at a time.'

In December 1992, John heard that one of his heroes, Geoff Capes, was doing a publicity show in Ripley, Derbyshire, UK. While in attendance, Geoff squeezed 24 bricks across his chest before they smashed to the floor.

'I thought about what I used to do when I was a brickie, and wondered if I'd still be able to do it,' says the father of two.

When he got home, to his amazement, he managed to balance 36 bricks on top of his head.

Since then, he's gone on to claim 28 world records, including his latest record attempt which involved balancing 92 people on his head – that's the equivalent of 5,180 kg (11,420 lb) – in one hour!

Over the years, John has thrown down the gauntlet, challenging anyone watching his act, offering a £2,000 reward to anyone who can match any part of his performance.

To date, no one has broken any of his records and, surprisingly, John has never broken his neck. 'I have never had an accident in all the while that I have been doing this. I think I have something of a gift.'

His softly spoken manner belies his 6 ft, 24½ stone frame, and he says that, although he enjoys the publicity, he tries to use it to good ends, raising more than £64,000 for charity.

## JOHN'S WORLD RECORDS INCLUDE:

### PINTS OF BEER
235 pints of beer balanced on his head, 15 November 2003.

## CANS OF COKE

428 cans of Coke (330ml cans) balanced on his head (total weight: 175 kg [385 lb]), 15 November 2003.

## BALANCING PEOPLE

John balanced 92 people on his head in an hour, 23 July 2000 at the Motorcycle Show, Lowestoft, UK.

## HOUSE BRICKS

101 house bricks balanced on the head (189 kg [416 lb]), 24 December 1997 on the National Lottery TV show, BBC, UK.

# FOOD, DRINK
# AND GASTRONOMIC
# RECORDS

## APPLE PIE

The world's largest apple pie was baked on 16 August 1997 in Wenatchee, Washington, USA. Co-ordinated by Keith Williams, director of the North Central Washington Museum, more than 600 volunteers gathered to help produce the pie, some helping with the peeling and slicing of 14,500 kg (32,000 lb) of apples, others, including a local American football team, kneading the dough. After 3 hours of labour, the grandiose concoction was cooked for more than 5 hours in a propane powered convection oven, which took form after a crane lifted a 3,000 m (10,000-ft) steel lid over the mixture-laden pan that measured 13.4 m by 7.3 m (44 x 24 ft). The American Pie weighed 15.37 tonnes (34,438 lb).

## BABY'S BOTTLE OF BEER

The landlord of Ye Old White Harte pub, in Hull, Humberside, UK, is a real sucker. Derrick Sykes holds the world record for the shortest time taken to drink half a pint of ale from a baby's bottle. On 19 April 1985, Derrick was timed at 3 minutes, 38.62 seconds.

## BAKED BEANS

Toilet attendant Kerry White holds the world record for the greatest number of baked beans consumed in 24 hours, with a total of 12,547. The beans were eaten individually with a cocktail stick and the record was created at Weymouth, Dorset, UK, on 20 August 1984.

During a radio broadcast on Radio Suffolk in June 2002, Dean Gould, of Felixstowe, Suffolk, UK, broke the record for eating the most individual baked beans in a minute using a cocktail stick with a total of 53.

On 4 April 1984, Karen Stevenson, of Wallasey, Merseyside, UK, ate 2,780 cold baked beans individually with a cocktail stick in the time of 30 minutes exactly.

## BANANAS

On 27 August 1987, Peter Dowdeswell, of Earls Barton, Northants, ate 17 peeled bananas in the record time of 1 minute, 47 seconds at TVS Studios, Southampton, UK

## BARREL OF BEER

The shortest recorded time in which a 9-gallon barrel of ale has been consumed is 2 hours, 14

minutes, 56.96 seconds by a team of 6: Derrick
Sykes (14), Alan Benstead (13), Chris Bentley (12),
Innis Belcher (11), Bill Simmons (11) and Dave
Watson (11) at Ye Olde White Harte pub, Hull,
Humberside, UK, on 27 May 1986. The figures in
brackets represent the number of pints consumed –
not their ages!

## BEER
Multi-record breaker Peter Dowdeswell, of Earls
Barton, Northamptonshire, UK, holds many eating
and drinking records, including a variety of beer
drinking records. See The Amazing... Peter
Dowdeswell section for further details.

### BEER THROUGH A STRAW
This category now relates to four different-sized
straws being used to drink a pint of beer in pubs
and clubs.
*3mm diameter:* 25.07 seconds by Peter Tyler at the
Ponsmere Hotel, Parranporth, Cornwall, UK, on 14
July 1983.
*4mm diameter:* 24.03 seconds by Tony Wildsmith at
the Catholic Club, Hoyland, Yorkshire, UK, on 18
April 1986.
*6mm diameter:* 11.60 seconds by Peter Dowdeswell at

the Boat Inn, Earls Barton, Northants, UK, on 14 March 1985.

*8mm diameter:* 9.63 seconds by Keith Medforth at the Four in Hand pub, Hull, Humberside, UK, on 21 February 1987.

## *BEER WITH A TEASPOON*

On 26 November 1985, Derrick Sykes drank a pint of beer with a teaspoon in 1 minute, 45.62 seconds on BBC TV's Breakfast Time. During the record-breaking attempt one of Derrick's front teeth was knocked out, witnessed by Chief scrutiniser, presenter Frank Bough. It just goes to show how serious record breaking is, and the lengths record breakers will go through to achieve their glory.

## BLACK PUDDING

On 1 August 1989, Billy (Bunter) Smith, of Croydon, Surrey, ate 1360 g (3 lb) of boiled black pudding in the record time of 7 minutes, 48.9 seconds.

## BLACK PUDDING – LONGEST

Eight butchers in the village of Bomal-sur-Ourthe, Belgium made the world's longest black pudding during February 2002. Using 3 tons of meat, 1 ton of onions and 1000 litres of blood, the black pudding had a length of 3,839 m (12,595 ft), and took 30 hours to prepare and cook. The sausage was cut into slices and sold off for charity.

## BOX OF CHOCOLATES

Department store chain Marshall Field's unveiled the world's largest box of chocolates on 14 November 2002 at the Field Museum in Chicago, USA. Measuring 4.6 m x 2.1 m x 0.6 m (15 ft x 7 ft x 2 ft) the over-sized Frango Win A Mint box contained 2,002 1 lb boxes of Frango Mint chocolates. The 908-kg (2,002-lb) box breaks the previous record of 856.4 m (1,888 lb).

## BRANDYSNAP

The fastest time that 900 g (2 lb) of Brandysnap has been consumed is 14 minutes, 10 seconds by Pauline Adams, of Winter, Hampshire, on 12 January 1990.

On 27 June 1988, a team of 4 bakers from Nottingham produced the world's largest brandysnap at exactly 5.5 m (18 ft).

## CABBAGE

At the 'Alternative Olympics' held in Hull, UK, on 12 June 1988, Andy Harper, of Scunthorpe,

Humberside, UK, devoured 1.3 kg (3 lb) of raw cabbage in the time of 26 minutes, 10 seconds.

## CAKE WITH MOST CANDLES
On 1 July 2004, people in Water Country, Portsmouth, lit 15,120 candles on a 12.2-m-long (40-ft-long) cake in honour of the 20th anniversary of Water Country.

## CARROTS
The fastest time ever recorded to munch through 1 kg (2.2 lb) of raw carrots is 10 minutes, 38.4 seconds by Marcel Leclerc, of Etaples, France, on 21 October 1989.

## CEREAL TREAT
Made with 1,680 boxes of Post Honey Bunches of Oats, Canadian cereal producer Post Cereals broke the world record for the largest cereal treat by producing a treat that weighed 1,315.40 kg (2,900 lb), beating the existing record of 1,025 kg (2,259.9 lb) held by an American team. The treat took 50 hours to make, and was unveiled at Toronto's Union Station on 1 June 2002, where it was shared with approximately 18,000 Torontonians.

## CHAMPAGNE

Multi-record breaker Peter Dowdeswell, of Earls Barton, Northamptonshire, UK, holds many eating and drinking records, including a variety of champagne drinking records. See The Amazing... Peter Dowdeswell section for further details.

## CHEESE

Peter Dowdeswell consumed 450 g (1 lb) of cheddar cheese in a time of 1 minute, 13 seconds on 13 July 1978.

## CHOCOLATE HEART

To celebrate Valentine's Day, online dating site Match.com unveiled the world's biggest chocolate heart on 13 February 2004. Designed by Lluis Morera, and using chocolate provided by Chocovic, Spain's largest chocolate producer, the gigantic sweet took the record by weighing 7 metric tons.

## CHOCOLATE SWEET

Presented at the festival Eurochocolate in Perugina, Italy, on 17 October 2003, Italy's most famous chocolate-maker Perugina revealed the world's largest chocolate sweet. Weighing 5,980 kg (13,193 lb), and taking more than 1,000 working hours to make, the chocolate sweet had a height of 2.15 m (7 ft), and a width of 2.31 m (7.57 ft)

## CIDER THROUGH A STRAW

The fastest recorded time that a pint of cider has been drunk through a straw (with a diameter of no more than 6mm) is 19.05 seconds by Derrick Sykes at Ye Olde White Harte pub, Hull, Humberside, UK, on 8 September 1985.

## COCKLES

Tony Dowdeswell, 19, downed two pints of cockles in 60.08 seconds at the Corby Stardust Bingo Hall on 14 February 1985.

## COCKTAIL

The biggest cocktail was made at Jimmy Buffett's Margaritaville Café in Universal Studios Citywalk, in Orlando, USA, on 18 May 2001. The Margarita Cocktail called 'Big Rita' was made with 4,900 L of tequila, lemon/lime juice and an orange-flavoured liqueur, and weighed 32 tonnes.

## COOKED MEAL

In February 2002, 140 people joined in to cook the world's largest meal, a big kabsa dish in the smallest

Arab country of Bahrain, using more than 5.5 tonnes of rice, meat, herbs, spices and tomatoes. Twenty cooks, aided by 120 helpers, poured 1,453 gallons of water into a specially built aluminium pot, then cooked 2.4 tonnes of basmati rice, 1.2 tonnes of meat and 1.94 tonnes of other ingredients and spices. The meal was left to cook for five hours in the park of the National Museum in Manama. The food was distributed to guests and to those in need, which included several thousand men, women and children who had gathered in festive mood for a taste.

## COOKIE

In Henderson, North Carolina, USA, the Immaculate Baking Company baked the world's largest cookie on 17 May 2003. Using a structureless oven, it utilised convective heat to bake the cookie within 6 hours. The cookie, measuring over 30.40 m (100 ft) in diameter and weighing 18,144 kg (40,000 lb), contained 13 million chunks of semi-sweet chocolate, 5.534 kg (12,200 lb) of unbleached flour, 30,000 whole eggs and 10 gallons of pure vanilla among other ingredients. Proceeds from the sale of the cookie were used to construct a Folk Art Museum.

## COUSCOUS

Students and teachers at a catering college in Tizi Ouzou, the main city in the north-eastern Kabylie region of Algeria, worked together to cook the world's biggest couscous. To make this mega version of the traditional north African dish, 2,600 kg (2.55 tons) of dry semolina (steamed and buttered), the meat of 100 sheep and 1524 kg (1.5 tons) of vegetables were used. A special couscoussior (traditional cooking pot) was constructed (4.3 m x 8 m [41.1 ft x 26.2 ft]) together with a specially built 3-tonne stove to cook it in. On completion, the couscous weighed 6,500 kg (14,300 lb), 4,500 kg (9920 lb) more than the previous record set in Tunisia. Organisers claimed that there was enough of the giant couscous to feed 22,000 guests.

## COTTAGE CHEESE

Dr Peter Altman, of Edgeware, Middlesex, UK, holds the world record for eating cottage cheese with a tablespoon. He gobbled down exactly 1.30 kg (3 lb) in 4 minutes on 4 March 1984.

Peter added to his record-breaking feats when he ate 250 g (8.83 oz) in 30 seconds on the Don't Miss Wax Show broadcast on Channel 4 on 20 June 1987.

## CRISPS

Dean Gould, of Felixstowe, Suffolk, UK, recorded a time of 4 minutes, 21 seconds in his attempt to consume six 20-g (0.71-oz) bags of crisps in the fastest time during a record festival held in July 2001.

## CUCUMBER

On 24 December 1988, Jens Rifsdal, of Aarhus, Denmark, consumed 1 kg (2.2 lb) of raw, unsliced cucumber in 4 minutes, 2.2 seconds.

## CURRY

A team of soldiers and an award-winning Indian restaurant chef cooked up the world's largest curry. Recruits from the Litchfield-based Army Training Regiment, together with British Curry Chef of the Year Abdul Salem, made the curry on 15 July 2000. Weighing just a little more than 3 tonnes, the gargantuan feast beats the previous best of 2,653 kg (5,849 lb) by nearly half a metric tonne. The recipe included 1,000 kg (2,204 lb) of potatoes, 50 kg (110 lb) of cauliflower, 50 kg (110 lb) of whole beans, 50 kg (110 lb) of carrots, 50 kg (110 lb) of cabbages, 2,300 L of plain yoghurt and 136 kg (300 lb) of spices – as well as several of Mr Salem's 'secret ingredients'. The record-breaking effort produced between 25,000 and 30,000 portions, and proceeds from the event – an estimated £60,000 – were donated afterwards to local charities.

## CUSTARD

At the Catholic Club, Hoyland, Yorkshire, UK, Alan Newbold drank four 1-pint mugs of cold custard in the record time of 1 minute, 36.05 seconds on 18 April 1986.

## DOGS' DINNER

On 8 September 1985, 506 dogs wolfed down 90 kg (200 lb) of meat and 45 kg (100 lb) of biscuits in exactly 10 minutes at Ragley Hall, Alcester, Warwickshire, UK.

## DOUGHNUTS

Twenty-stone miner Patrick Cunnade, of Wakefield, UK, scoffed 20 113.4-g (4-oz) doughnuts in exactly 6 minutes on 13 October 1987.

Peter Dowdeswell ate 45 two-hole, 155.9-g (5.5-oz) doughnuts in 17 minutes, 32 seconds in New York, USA, on 12 August 1983.

On 5 March 2004, Ray Meduna (USA) ate 22 42.5-g (1½ oz) doughnuts in 1 minute, 39 seconds at KISW radio in Seattle, USA. He followed the rules of the International Federation of Competitive Eating which allow the doughnuts to be dipped into water before eating.

## EELS

The fastest recorded time that 1 pint (approx. 1,000 elvers, total weight approx. 900 g [2 lb]) of eels have been downed is 32.21 seconds by Mark Ryder, 26, of Frampton on Severn, UK, at the annual World Championships at Gloucestershire, UK, on 20 April 1987.

Peter Dowdeswell has downed 450 g (1 lb) of elvers in 13.7 seconds.

## EGGS

*RAW*

50 from 4 1-pint mugs in 28.20 seconds by Alan Newbold at the Catholic Club, Hoyland, UK, on 21 April 1984.

30 from 2 1-pint mugs in 10.30 seconds by Alan Newbold at the Catholic Club, Hoyland, UK, on 17 May 1985.

36 from a 'yard of ale' glass in 17.08 seconds by Alan Newbold at the Catholic Club, Hoyland, UK, on 21 June 1986.

*HARD BOILED*

14 in 14.42 seconds by John Kenmuir of Hamilton, Lanarkshire, UK, on Scottish TV's Live at 1.30 programme on 17 April 1987.

65 in 6 minutes, 40 seconds (without a drink) by Sonya Thomas.

## FISH AND CHIPS

Peter Dowdeswell ate 1.8 kg (4 lb) of fish plus 1.81 kg (4 lb) of chips in 5 minutes, 42 seconds at the Top Rank Club, Dudley, West Midlands, UK, on 14 May 1976.

Londoner Geoffrey Smith, 75, makes a 23-km (14.3-mile) round trip to his favourite chip shop every evening so that he can eat the dish he has eaten every night for more than 40 years. Father of five Smith has eaten over 14,000 portions of battered and deep-fried fish along with fried chips ever since he joined a pub darts team in his mid-thirties.

The largest portion of fish and chips was served at The Black Rose public house, in Boston, Massachusetts, USA, on 15 March 2004. Organised by a leading seafood manufacturer, the new world record of 35.27 kg (77.75 lb) – 15.56 kg (34.31 lb) of battered and fried cod fillet and 19.75 kg (43.54

lb) of chips – beats the previous record of 32.65 kg (71.99 lb) held by a South African establishment.

## FRUIT AND VEGETABLE CARVING DISPLAY

Wang Xiang of China and his team of 29 assembled the biggest fruit and vegetable carving display in the world in November 2003 at the 'Guests 2003' fair held in Leipzig (Germany). Consisting of 34 different fruits and vegetables, the buffet measured 6.60 m (21.65 ft) in length, 2.05 m (6.72 ft) in width and 2.35 m (7.7 ft) in height.

## GHERKINS

Peter Dowdeswell ate 450 g (1 lb) of gherkins in 27.2 seconds.

## GINGERBREAD TOWN

The German city of Rostock, much of which was destroyed during Allied bombings in World War II, was recreated entirely in gingerbread in December 2002, by Sven Grumbach, a local strawberry farm and sweet shop owner. Grumbach used pictures from a 16th-century scroll that managed to survive the war as a guideline to recreate the city, making hundreds of cookie houses, covering more than 330 sq m (400 sq yd). Using a traditional recipe, the quantity of ingredients is impressive, including 798 kg (1,760 lb) of flour, 320 kg (705 lb) of honey, 399 kg (880 lb) of almonds, 79 kg (175 lb) of raisins and 2,400 eggs to complete the project.

## GRAPES
Multi-record holder Peter Dowdeswell ate a 1.36-kg (3-lb) bunch of grapes (still attached to stalks) in 31.1 seconds.

## HAMBURGERS
Peter Dowdeswell ate 21 hamburgers, each 100 g (3.5 oz) in weight, including buns, in 9 minutes, 42 seconds at Cockshut Hill School, Yardley, Birmingham, UK, on 30 June 1984.

Since 1972, Don Gorske, of Fond du Lac, Wisconsin, USA, has eaten Big Macs every day – and as many as nine in a day! To date, he has eaten more than 18,000 of the famous burger sandwiches, and students at Fond du Lac High School have calculated that, over the years, Gorske has eaten 800 heads of lettuce, 820 onions, 1,900 whole pickles, 255.4 kg (563 lb) of cheese, 100 gallons of special sauce, 14½ cows and 6.25 million sesame seeds.

## HOT CROSS BUNS

On 9 April 1971, during the interlude at a pop concert in Cathedral Square, Peterborough, UK, Walter Cornelius ate 10 283.5-g (10-oz) hot cross buns in 5 minutes, 10 seconds.

The female record for eating five 283.5-g (10-oz) hot cross buns is held by Gillian Clark, of Hull, Humberside, UK, with a time of 4 minutes, 53.6 seconds, set on Radio Humberside's 'Chris Bell' show on 14 April 1987.

## HOT DOGS

*MOST EATEN*

Takeru Kobayashi of Japan – the Michael Jordan of hot dog eating – broke his own record on 4 July 2004 when he gobbled 53½ frankfurters in just 12 minutes. The reed-thin Kobayashi ploughed through an average of one hot dog every 13.5 seconds to ensure he would retain the mustard-yellow championship belt in the 89th competition at Nathan's Famous in Coney Island. At 1.7 m (5 ft 7 in), Kobayashi was one of the lightest of the competitors, weighing in at 51.25 kg (113 lb).

On the same occasion, Sonya Thomas (USA) broke the women's record by eating 32 hot dogs.

*LARGEST*

The world's largest hot dog was created in Radford City, Virginia, USA, under the direction of Jack Sharlow and with the help of the Radford University catering team. The hot dog, measuring 6.95 m (22 ft 8 in) long and 12.7 cm (5 in) wide, began with over 92 m (300 ft) of casing from sausage links, which was then filled with smaller ground up hot dogs. The team used a blowtorch to cook the hot dog, which took almost 4 hours to complete. But no hot dog is complete without its obligatory bun. The bun took a few hours to mix up, allowing for the dough to rise and for the team to roll out. It took a further 11 hours to bake. To complete the large hot dog a dressing was required, and for the finishing touches four bottles of ketchup and mustard were used, together with four jars of relish and a dozen diced onions. The hot dog was presented at the Memorial Bridge Farewell Picnic in the summer of 2002. Although no one was allowed to eat the hot dog, due to a request from the local health inspector, it was enjoyed by all.

## ICE LOLLY

Residents of the Dutch seaside town of Katwijk aan de Rijn were witness to the world's largest ever ice lolly in 1997. The ice cream measured 7 m (23 ft) high and weighed 9,150 kg (20,172 lb). Exhibited at an event, which was covered on national television and watched by over 20,000 people, the ice lolly was the brainchild of Unilever's Dutch ice cream company Iglo-Ola. The company decided to build a giant record-breaking version of their successful 'Raket' ice cream. Built at the Iglo–Ola ice cream plant at Hellendoorn, it took a team of 17 people three weeks to freeze the mixture at a temperature of -25°c. The massive mould for the ice cream also took a week to produce.

## JAM
Schwartau (a German jam producer) and Schott Glass company, of Germany, made the biggest jar of jam in 1989. A glass jar standing 1.54 m (5 ft) tall, with a diameter of 97 cm (38 in), and weighing 98 kg (216 lb) empty, was filled with 1,054 kg (2,324 lb) of jam. It took 1½ years to make the glass jar.

## JELLY
Peter Dowdeswell ate 0.6 L (20 fl oz) of set jelly in 8.25 seconds at the Royal Oak, Bishops Cleeve, Gloucestershire, UK, on 5 July 1986.

## LAGER THROUGH A STRAW

This category now relates to four different-sized straws being used in pubs and clubs.

*3mm diameter:* 32.39 seconds by Derrick Sykes at BBC TV's Pebble Mill Studios, Birmingham, UK, on 19 November 1985.

*4mm diameter:* 28.62 seconds by Alex Liddle at Patrington Haven, Humberside, UK, on 9 July 1986.

*6mm diameter:* 11.50 seconds by Peter Hanson at Birmingham Students' Carnival, Birmingham, UK, on 16 November 1985.

*8mm diameter:* 11.02 seconds by Horace Forge at The Red Lion, Norwich, Norfolk, UK, on 17 April 1986.

## LAGER WITH A TEASPOON

At Birmingham Students' Carnival Rag on 16 November 1985, Steve Stringer, UK, set a new lager drinking record by slurping down a pint of lager with a teaspoon in 3 minutes, 36 seconds.

## LATTE

In celebration of the launch of a new latte range, Nestle produced a record-breaking latte to beat the previous record of 329.95 gallons held in Verona, Italy. Using 215.5 kg (475 lb) of vanilla-flavoured

Nestle Coffee-Mate Latte Creations, 20.4 kg (45 lb) of Nescafe Taster's Choice and nearly 500 gallons of water, the world's largest latte was unveiled on 13 May 2004 in New York's Greeley Square, USA. The 660.5-gallon latte measured 2.1 m high x 1.8 m wide (7-ft x 6-ft) and weighed 2268 kg (5,000 lb), and would take the average American coffee drinker nine years to consume.

## LOLLIPOP

More than 50 employees of the American confectionery giant Hershey Foods Corporation worked together for over 3 months to design and build the world's largest Jolly Rancher lollipop. Weighing a staggering 1,828 kg (4,031 lb) with the stick (or 1,821 kg [4,016 lb] without stick), and measuring 1.6 m (5.23 ft) in diameter (without stick), and 4.8 m (15.9 ft) tall with stick. The cherry flavoured lollipop measured 48 cm (18.9 in) thick, and was created to celebrate the launch of a new range of Jolly Rancher lollipops, and was unwrapped at The Taste of Chicago, USA on 30 June 2002.

## MILK

Peter Dowdeswell drank 2 pints of milk in 3.2 seconds at the Top Rank Club, Dudley, West Midlands, UK, on 31 May 1975.

## MILK RICE

To mark the eighth anniversary of Sri Lankan *Sirasa* Radio, 183-m-long (600-ft-long), 0.76-m-wide (2-½-ft) wide 'kiribath' (milk rice) was cooked in Colombo, Sri Lanka, using 2,000 coconuts, and 1,000 kg (2,204 lb) of boiled white rice. One hundred and fifty cooks led by Publis Silva, Head Chef of the Mount Lavinia Hotel, worked to make the giant preparation.

## MUSTARD

Wally Sharpless scoffed a 170-g (6-oz) jar of English mustard in a world record time of 8 minutes, 42 seconds at King's Lynn, Norfolk, on 13 March 1989.

## OLIVES

Constantine Hadgipatterus of Yannina, Greece, is the world champion olive eater, with a tally of 150 (stoned and stuffed) in 16 minutes, 02.2 seconds achieved on 17 February 1986.

## OMELETTE

In Brockville, Ontario, Canada, on 11 May 2002, more than 200 people took part in an effort to make the world's biggest omelette. Using a specially constructed frying pan that measured 141.4 sq m (1,520 sq ft), local chefs, hospitality students and local residents got together to mix the giant omelette using 46,000 eggs, 136 kg of tomatoes, 136 kg (300 lb) of onions and 72.5 kg (160 lb) of green peppers. When finally cooked, the giant omelette measured 141.4 sq m (1,520 sq ft). The titan's breakfast took hours longer to cook, and beat a previous record that was held in Japan.

## ONIONS

On 18 December 1979, Walter Cornelius, of Peterborough, Cambridgeshire, UK, shattered the world record for eating raw onions by downing 1.72 kg (3 lb 8 oz) in 2 minutes, 2 seconds.

## ORANGE JUICE, GLASS OF

The world's largest glass of orange stands 2.59 m (8.5 ft) tall, with a diameter of nearly 1.50 m (5 ft). On 22 April 1998, in honour of National Minority Cancer Awareness week, the glass was exhibited in a Seattle, Washington, USA, grocery store, and filled with 730 gallons of Florida Valencia orange juice, weighing a total of 3,628 kg (8,000 lb). The glass took two weeks to build, and has a refrigerator unit built into the glass to keep the orange juice cool at 35 degrees.

## PANCAKES
Peter Dowdeswell ate 62 15.20-cm (6-inch) diameter pancakes with syrup in 6 minutes, 58.5 seconds at the Dropey, Northampton, UK, on 9 February 1977.

## PASTA – LARGEST BOWL
In August 2002, Nintendo, the computer games console manufacturer, organised a promotional stunt for its forthcoming Super Mario Sunshine game and dished up 1,481 kg (3,265 lb) of 'pasta à la Mario' in a 0.91-m-high x 3.04-m-wide (3-ft x 10-ft) bowl. The previous world record for the largest bowl of pasta weighed 1,163 kg (2,564 lb).

## PIE
Up to 50,000 people had a slice of the world's biggest pie when it was unveiled in Denby Dale, West Yorkshire, UK, on 2 September 2000. The Denby Dale Pie, as it is affectionately known, is the

tenth biggest pie to have been made in the region since the event started in 1788 with the King George III pie to celebrate the monarch's return to sanity (though temporary). The latest pie weighed 12 tonnes, and was baked in a 12.2-m-long x 2.74-m-wide x 0.91-m-deep (40-ft x 9-ft x 3-ft) dish. A blanket of shortcrust pastry weighing 3,465 kg (7,639 lb) covered the filling which included 5,000 kg (11,023 lb) of British beef, 2,000 kg (4,409 lb) of potatoes, 1,000 kg (2,205 lb) of onions and 100 kg (220 lb) of John Smith's Bitter. Former Coldstream Guard Raymond Haigh, 70, was in charge of the security of the pie. His role as The Guardian of the Pie gave him the opportunity to have a mouthful of it before anyone else.

## PINEAPPLE

The fastest recorded time for eating a 32-oz (2-lb) pineapple, skin and all (but not the green top), is 3 minutes, 33.4 seconds, by Dave Walton, of Newcastle, Tyne and Wear, UK, on 17 December 1974.

## PIZZA

World champion pizza eater and record holder is John Kenmuir, of Hamilton, UK, who munched his way through a 0.9 kg (2-lb) pizza in the time of exactly 29 seconds at the Glasgow Garden Festival on 12 August 1988.

## POPCORN BOX

Espahle, a Brazilian popcorn company, claimed the world record for the largest box of popcorn in July 2003 when they made a 13ft 8inch (4.2 m) tall box and filled it with 23 cubic m (812.13 cubic ft) of popcorn in Porto Alegre.

## POPCORN CONE

On 7 December 1997, the people of Velbert-Tönisheide of Germany broke the world record for the longest popcorn cone with a measure of 50 m (164 ft), beating the old Swiss record by 4.5 m (14.76 ft). After the world record was established, small portions of the giant cone were sold, with proceeds going to benefit handicapped children in Velbert-Tönisheide.

## PORRIDGE

Peter Dowdeswell ate 2.72 kg (6 lb) of porridge in 2 minutes, 34 seconds at Earls Barton, Northants, UK, on 2 July 1977.

## PORTER
Walter Cornelius drank 3 consecutive 3-pint 'yards' of porter in 39.9 seconds at the Dolphin, Peterborough, UK, on 20 September 1971.

## POTATOES
Peter Dowdeswell ate 1.36 kg (3 lb) of mashed potatoes in 1 minute, 22 seconds at Earls Barton, Northants, UK, on 25 August 1978.

## POTATO CHIPS
On 8 August 2003, workers from five Ohio-based potato-chip companies and the Agriculture Department spent almost 8 hours slicing, frying and salting 288,000 chips made from more than 2 tons of potatoes in their attempt to set the record for the biggest bag of potato chips in the world. Local companies contributed by donating equipment and ingredients, including 318 kg (700 lb) of soybean oil and 36 kg (80 lb) of salt. In front of spectators at the Ohio State Fair, the crowd applauded as the bag was filled and the scales edged past the half-ton mark, finally stopping at 491 kg (1,082.5 lb) when the bag was sealed. Not for someone on a diet, the bag of chips contained 160,000 g (353 lb) of fat and 2.5 million calories.

## POTATO SALAD

A giant potato salad produced in Latvia by Spilva, a food and vegetable processing company, to mark its 10th anniversary, is the biggest of its kind and was made with every ingredient being cut by hand. The 3,277-kg (7,224-lb) potato salad, called rasols, is a favourite dish in Latvia, and is traditionally served at celebrations. The record-breaking dish, served late in 2002, consisted of boiled potatoes, boiled carrots, sausage, boiled eggs, green peas, pickled cucumbers and dressed with sour cream and mayonnaise. The meal was dished up to 4,500 people, taking an astonishing 30 minutes to devour the lot!

## PRUNES

The most prodigious feat of prune eating was performed by Alan Newbold of Barnsley, UK, who demolished 150 with a tablespoon in exactly 31 seconds at Bassets, Sheffield, Yorkshire, UK, on 4 February 1984.

## RAISINS

On 16 December 1986, Rasmus Rifsdal, of Copenhagen, Denmark, ate 100 raisins individually with a cocktail stick, in the record time of 42.5 seconds. The following day, Rasmus set another world record when he ate 200 raisins in similar fashion in 2 minutes, 03.78 seconds.

## RAVIOLI

Peter Dowdeswell ate 2.26 kg (5 lb) of Ravioli (170 pieces) in 5 minutes, 34 seconds at Pleasurewood Hills American Theme Park, Lowestoft, Suffolk, UK, on 25 September 1983.

## RICE

Goanese merchant seaman Parbatinath Basu is the world champion boiled rice eater. At Visakapatnam, India, on 24 December 1970, he downed 1.27 kg (2 lb 8 oz) in 17 minutes, 11 seconds, using only his fingers – and left not one solitary grain.

## SANDWICH

Twenty-four bakers in Mexico City surprised onlookers who watched awe-struck in Zocolo Square as they made the world's largest sandwich. The giant creation weighed 2,403 kg (5,297 lb) and measured 3.48 sq m (11 sq ft 5 in). Made by Grupo Bimbo and associates, the special sarnie contained ham, cheese, lettuce and mayonnaise, and eventually, after the excitement of what they had achieved had died down, was shared by the bakers, not one of them having a big enough appetite to stomach the whole sandwich individually!

## SAUSAGES

The greatest number of cooked 28.35-g (1-oz) sausages consumed in 1 hour is 122.5 by Joe Blackie of Edinburgh, UK, at his local pub, The Norhet, on 14 January 1983.

The following sausage-eating records are all held by the late Walter Cornelius of Peterborough, Cambridgeshire, UK.

47 2-oz (56.7 g) *(raw)* in 8 minutes, 30 seconds at Cathedral Square, Peterborough, UK, on 11 April 1972.

30 2-oz (56.7 g) *(hot)* in 10 minutes, 11.8 seconds at Peterborough Motor Show Rooms, UK, on 8 May 1969.

5.36-m (17 ft 6 in) chain of raw 56.7 g (2-oz) sausages (total weight 2.26 kg [5 lb]) in 5 minutes, 34 seconds at Peterborough Municipal Swimming Baths, UK, on 22 June 1979.

## SPAGHETTI

The fastest recorded time for consuming 114 m (125 yd) of spaghetti plus sauce from a 4-pint container is 8.61 seconds by Alan Newbold of

Barnsley, at Ye Olde White Harte, Hull, Humberside, UK, on 2 April 1986.

## SPINACH

The greatest spinach-eating marathon ever undertaken was one of 6 hours, at Havirov, Czechoslovakia, during which time Josef Peltzner, of Czechoslovakia, munched his way through 6.322 kg (13.93 lb).

## SPRING ROLL

It took 45 minutes for 270 chefs and 130 hospital workers and volunteers to roll the biggest Chinese spring roll in the world. The record-breaking poh piah measured 206.32 m long and was prepared and presented at the Changi General Hospital, Changi, Singapore on 8 June 2004. After the event, the poh piah was cut up into pieces, half of which were sold for $2 a piece to raise $2,784 for the hospital's home-care assistance scheme.

## SPROUTS

On 21 October 1987, Terry Smith ate 1.36 g (3 lb) of cooked Brussels sprouts using only a knitting needle, in the record time of 18 minutes, 10 seconds at the Minerva Tavern, Hull, Humberside, UK.

The female record is held by Dianne Core, who scoffed 900 g (2 lb) in 16 minutes, 20 seconds at the 'Alternative Olympics' held in Hull, UK on 12 June 1988.

## STRAWBERRIES
Peter Dowdeswell ate 900 g (2 lb) of strawberries in 12.95 seconds at Easby Street, Nottingham, UK, on 5 July 1985.

## STRAWBERRY CAKE
The longest strawberry cake was prepared by 74 chefs from a cookery club in Leipzig, Germany. It was 104.16 m (677 ft) long. The ingredients included 150 kg (331 lb) strawberries, 30 kg (66.1 lb) jam, 48 L (101 pints) of whipped cream and 6 kg (13.2 lb) pistachios. The record–breaking cake was made on 19 June 2004 at Belantis amusement park near Leipzig.

## SUET PUDDING
2 kg (4.5 lb) of suet pudding topped with a half gallon of custard was the dessert served up to Alan Newbold, of Barnsley, Yorkshire, UK, at The Drop, Addiston. Alan gobbled up the lot in 18 minutes exactly on 17 July 1983.

## SUSHI

Peter Dowdeswell ate (0.68 kg) (1.5 lb) of Sushi (raw fish and rice) in 1 minute, 13.5 seconds in Tokyo, Japan, on 22 February 1985.

## SUSHI ROLL

1,400 kg rice was used to make the longest sushi roll. It was a 1,335.25-m-long (4,381-ft-long) cucumber roll, made in Ichinoseki City, Japan, on 10 August 2001. The roll was consumed by 2,600 people.

## SULTANAS

The fastest recorded time in which 100 sultanas have been devoured, singly, using only a cocktail stick, is 1 minute, 44.65 seconds by Mark Say of Selly Oak, Birmingham, UK, on 16 November 1985.

## SWEETCORN

The maximum number of individual sweetcorn kernels ever picked from a plate and eaten within 1 minute is 41. Multi-record holder Dean Gould set this record during a record exhibition in Felixstowe, Suffolk, UK, during July 2001.

## TACO

Eight thousand hungry supporters watched on in Monterrery, Mexico, as a group of Mexican restaurateurs created the world's largest taco. Felipe Rodriguez, one of the restaurant owners, said on beating the existing record held in Texas, USA, 'The taco is a symbol of Mexico; it's not possible that the United States hold this record.' The taco, made from 10,000 wheat tortillas stuck together, and filled with meat, cheese and onion, weighed a monster 596.9 kg (94 stone) and measured 15 m (49 ft) in length.

## TORTILLA

In April 2000, residents of the colonial city of Oaxaca (pronounced Wah-ha-ka) in Mexico celebrated its 468th anniversary by making a 4.27-m (14-ft) tortilla, the largest ever made. The massive meal was topped with 31.75 kg (70 lb) of cheese, 31.75 kg (70 lb) of beef, 20.41 kg (45 lb) of beans and 5 gallons of salsa.

## VEGETABLES

John Evans, of Palmer, Alaska, USA, holds countless records, including seven world records for growing large vegetables. The following are his world records:

*Broccoli (Romanesco):* weighing 15.87 kg (35 lb).
*Carrot:* weighing 8.6 kg (18.985 lb).
*Kohlrabi:* weighing 17.9 kg (39.5 lb).
*Red Cabbage:* weighing 20.5 kg (45.25 lb).
*Kale:* weighing 12.7 kg (28 lb).

## WATERMELONS

The fastest recorded time for eating five watermelons (total weight 3175 kg [7 lb] is 8 minutes, 30 seconds by Reg Morris (UK) at The Woolpack, Short Heath, West Midlands, UK, on 4 September 1985.

## WEDDING CAKE

Made to celebrate Holland's royal wedding of Crown Prince Willem-Alexander to Mazima Zorreguita, the world's biggest wedding cake was displayed in the market town of Ommen in February 2002. Measuring 18 m (59 ft) high, and weighing 5,000 kg (11,023 lb), it took 75 cooks more than three weeks to prepare, and a day to decorate. Due to the time it had taken to make, and the fact that it was on public display, health inspectors ruled that the cake was unfit for eating. The giant cake broke the previous record of 2.74 m (9 ft), weighing 693 kg (1,527.8 lb) set by

Serendipity Three restaurant, New York, USA, in February 2001.

## YORKSHIRE PUDDING

John Davidson, 29, of Gainsborough, Lincolnshire, UK, laid claim to a new world record for eating Yorkshire Pudding by wolfing 1.36 kg (3 lb) plus half a pint of onion gravy in 7 minutes, 22 seconds on 18 March 1986.

# THE AMAZING ...
# PETER DOWDESWELL

*'The reason I drink beer so quickly is
that I can't stand the taste...'*
Peter Dowdeswell

Peter Dowdeswell has a healthy appetite for most things in life and, like most of us, enjoys the occasional drink and loves his food. Unlike most of us, however, Peter also happens to be the gastronomic champion, the man with the single most eating and drinking records ever held.

In 1974, Peter began his phenomenal record-breaking career by downing a 3-pint yard of ale in an incredible 5.4 seconds. Since then, he has travelled the world breaking one record after another and, like many of our amazing record holders, has raised several thousand pounds for charity along the way.

By 1979, Peter had accumulated many world records, consuming gallons of beer and amazing everyone from fellow record holders to doctors. In October of that year, Peter agreed to take part in a scientific experiment, and was subjected to rigorous and exacting tests by the medical profession. It was hoped they might discover why he never showed any signs of drunkenness after consuming so much alcohol during his world record-breaking feats, and by using Peter as a 'guinea pig' they might find a cure for alcoholism.

Peter drank 4 pints of beer during an hour and was given a breathalyser test. The meter reading (50)

indicated that his blood/alcohol level equated to the same as if he had consumed only one and a half pints of beer. During the next four hours Peter was asked to consume a further 21 pints of beer, which he obligingly did. This brought the total consumed to

25 pints in five hours. After every five pints, Peter was given a breathalyser test and blood test. The meter reading of 50 never varied and the blood analysis confirmed that according to science he had only consumed the equivalent alcohol contained in one and a half pints of beer.

Undeterred, the scientists decided to try again to get Peter drunk and, later during the same month, he was subjected to what must surely be the ultimate in medical research in alcohol consumption. Using the same methods as before and treble-checking all the equipment and findings, Peter consumed 76 pints of beer inside 16 hours of testing. On each and every occasion the result was the same. The instruments and blood analysis showed a blood/alcohol level equivalent to Peter only having consumed one and a half pints of beer.

It is not known exactly how far the team of scientists has progressed since their findings were made public. However, it's a fair bet they are still as baffled as ever.

Peter believes that his only key to success is his determination, hard work and constant practice. 'The reason I drink beer so quickly is that I can't stand the taste,' he quips. Odd as that might sound, it's perfectly true, Peter is a tee totaller and drinks only soft drinks when he's down his local pub in Earls Barton, UK, unless he's breaking records.

The 6 ft 1 in, 16.5-stone quietly spoken Cockney has answered the challenge of would-be pretenders to his crown. All have been beaten into obscurity but all will remember Peter Dowdeswell.

## PETER'S WORLD RECORDS INCLUDE:

### DRINKING
1 pint of beer in 0.45 seconds
1 litre of beer upside down in 6 seconds
1 litre of beer consumed in 1.30 seconds
2 pints of beer in 2.30 seconds
2 pints of beer upside down in 6.4 seconds
2½-pint 'yard of ale' in 4.9 seconds
3-pint 'yard of ale' in 5 seconds
3 pints of beer in 4.2 seconds
4-pint 'yard of ale' in 8.90 seconds
4 pints of beer upside down in 22.1 seconds
2 litres of beer in 6 seconds
2 litres of beer upside down in 14.6 seconds
5-pint 'yard of ale' in 10 seconds
5 pints of beer upside down in 29 seconds
7½-pint 'yard of ale' in 14 seconds
1 gallon of beer upside down in 8 minutes, 35 seconds

1 pint of champagne upside down in 3.3 seconds
3½-pint 'yard of champagne' in 14.2 seconds
2 pints of milk in 3.2 seconds
34 pints of beer in 1 hour
90 pints of beer in 3 hours

## EATING

Jelly – 18 fl oz in solidified form with a spoon in 22.34 seconds

Meat pies – 22 156-g (5.5-oz) meat pies in 18 minutes, 13.3 seconds

Cheese – 454 g (1 lb) of cheddar in 1 minute, 13 seconds

Grapes – 1.36 kg (3 lb) bunch (still attached to stalks) in 31.1 seconds

Gherkins – 454 g (1 lb) in 27.2 seconds

Shrimps – 1.36 kg (3 lb) in 4 minutes, 8 seconds

Mashed potato – 1.36 kg (3 lb) in 1 minute, 22 seconds

Eggs, raw – 13 in 1.04 seconds

Eggs, hard boiled – 14 in 14.42 seconds

Porridge – 2.72 kg (6 lb) in 2 minutes, 34 seconds

Haggis – 737.5 g (1 lb 10 oz) in 49 seconds

Ice cream (partly thawed) – 5.44 kg (12 lb) in 45.5 seconds

Strawberries – 907 g (2 lb) in 12.95 seconds

# SPORTING
# RECORDS

## AEROBATICS – LOOPING THE LOOP

The oldest flight passenger to fly a loop is Adeline Ablitt, UK, who at 95 looped the loop as a passenger of a glider in 1998.

## BACKWARDS RUNNING

These distance records are for running backwards:

*MEN*

200 m: Roland Wegner (Germany), 32.38 sec, 13 June 2004, Hof/Saale, Germany.

400 m: Thomas Dold (Germany), 1:14 min, 20 June 2004, Gengenbach, Germany.

800 m: Thomas Dold (Germany), 2:40 min, 20 June 2004, Gengenbach, Germany (beating the previous record of 2:50.4 min by Brian Godsey (USA), established just 5 days before).

4 x 100 m Relay: Jos Cammaerts, Stefaan Sonck, Yvon Sonck, Chris Van San (Belgium), 1:17.70 min, 27 June 2003, Brussels.

Half Mile: Ronald Provenzano (USA), 3:23 min, 2003, Long Island.

1000 m: Thomas Dold (Germany), 3:35 min, 21 February 2004, Augsburg, Germany.

1500 m: Thomas Dold (Germany), 5 minutes, 55 seconds on 7 May 2004 in Weiz (Austria).

2,000 m: Stefano Morselli (Italy), 8:36 min, 27 Sept 2003, Camaiore, Italy.

3,000 m: Brian Godsey (USA), 11:54 min, 3 July 2004, Poviglio, Italy.

5,000 m: Bud Badyna (USA), 21:50.6 min, 3 August 1991, Oregon, USA.

Half Marathon: Yves Pol (France), 1:42 hrs, 1989.

Marathon: Bud Badyna (USA), 3:53:17 hrs, 24 April 1994, Toledo, USA.

*WOMEN*

400 m: Karien Coppens (Netherlands), 1:45.65 min, 9 May 2002.

4 x 100 m: Hilde Meesters, Stephany Baxter, Annmieke Demaeghdt and Edith Grollé, 1:48.79 min, 28 June 2002, Belgium.

1,000 m: Stefania Zambello (Italy), 4:20 min, 1 March 2003, Augsburg, Germany.

1 Mile: Stefania Zambello (Italy), 7:34 min, in 1998.

2,000 m: Ann Ebner (Germany), 12:31.6 min, 27 July, Hamburg, Germany.

3,000 m: Stefania Zambello (Italy), 13:42 min, 3 July 2004, Poviglio, Italy.

## BALL KICKING

On 17 February 1974, Robert Smith, 23, of South Cave, East Yorkshire, UK, kicked a standard leather match play football 64.5 m (212 ft) from a spot kick to first bounce. (N. B. This record was not wind assisted.)

## BARREL LIFTING

Fritz Konrad, of Austria (national weight lifting champion), lifted a barrel weighing 158 kg (348 lb).

## BASKETBALL – BLINDFOLDED!

The fastest recorded time to achieve 10 baskets while totally blindfolded is 2 minutes, 42 seconds by Sadie Edwards, of Birmingham, UK, on television show You Bet, screened on 16 February 1989 in the UK.

## BASKETBALL

### 24-HOUR DRIBBLING

On 16–17 December 2003, ultra-marathon runner Tyler Curiel broke the record for dribbling a basketball while running over a 24-hour period. The event called 'Bounce for Life' to support research in Curiel's lab at Tulane University School of Medicine, New Orleans, USA, where he is the chief of haematology and medical oncology, saw him surpass the existing record with a distance of 177.44 km (108.4 miles).

## MOST BASKETS BY HEADING BALL

The most consecutive baskets achieved by heading the ball is 17 by Jacek Roszkowski of Poland. This record was set in Dessau at the 2001 Saxonia record festival. The ball did not touch the ground or any other body part other than the head.

## ENTERTAINMENT

Joseph Odhiambo, a native of Nairobi, Kenya (now living in the USA), is the holder of two very different basketball records. His first record is for dribbling 6 basketballs simultaneously with hands and feet for a period of no less than 1 minute. His second record is for juggling 3 basketballs while shooting 43 lay-ups in one minute.

## BENCH PRESS

The following are for the most repetitions lifted in 30 minutes:

50 kg x 1,107 repetitions by Karl-Eugen Reck, of Germany, on 27 April 1996.

40 kg x 1,435 repetitions by Karl-Eugen Reck, of Germany, on 27 May 1984.

A team of 4 lifted a combined weight of 204,320 kg (450,448 lb) on 12 October 1985. (The team consisted of Jürgen Boss, Bülent Isgören, Karl-Eugen Reck and Michael Zeiler.)

## CARROM – THE FASTEST PLAYER
In his home town of Bangalore, India, Professor S. Ramesh Babulore pocketed all 19 carrom pawns in the record time of 39.61 seconds on 21 November 1999.

## CHIN-UPS
On 26 October 2002, 38-year-old former marine Alan Sharkany set the record for completing the most chin-ups in 24 hours. Sharkany of Milford, Connecticut, USA, set out to complete 4,000 chin-ups, however managed 2,101 before retiring due to an injury to his left bicep.

The most chin-ups on a bar without leaving the hanging position is 442 in 2 hours, 15 minutes by Bui Anh Nghe, during a contest in the army of Vietnam at Haiphong on 22 December 1986.

The most chin-ups done in 3 minutes is 100 by Ngo Xuan Chuyen (Vietnam) in 1988.

The record for the most chin-ups in 1 minute belongs to Jean-François Huette of France who lifted himself up 37 times.

## COMPACT DISC THROWING

On 11 July 1998, Kim Flatow from Germany, threw a compact disc a distance of 66.75 m (218.99 ft) during the Flensburg World Record Festival in Flensburg, Germany.

## CYCLING, ARTISTIC

Martina Štěpánková (Czech Republic) has a world record for cycling a distance of 31.25 m (102.5 ft) – not in the usual way but by standing on hands (one hand on the saddle, the other one at the handle bar).

## CYCLING BACKWARDS

Christian Patzig of Lübeck, Germany, learned cycling at the age of four and started playing the violin in 1970. Since then, he has combined the two to set and break world records for cycling backwards. His current world record for cycling backwards with a violin is 60.45 km (37.56 miles) in 5 hours, 9 minutes.

On 24 May 2003, Markus Riese of Germany broke the distance record for riding a bicycle backwards in an hour when he achieved a distance of 29.1 km (18 miles). He continued cycling until he broke the 50-km record (31 miles), recording a world record time of 1 hour, 46 minutes, 59 seconds.

## CYCLING BACKWARDS, 100 KM

On 11 August 1985, Alan Pierce, of Australia, rode a cycle backwards over the distance of 100 km (62 miles), setting a record time of 4 hours, five minutes, 1 second.

## CYCLING BACKWARDS, LONGEST DISTANCE

During 1992 in Lucani, Serbia, Goran Alempijevic, of Serbia, rode a cycle backwards 147.15 km (91.43 miles) in 6½ hours.

## CYCLING, FASTEST

Fred Rompelberg, of the Netherlands, rode a bicycle at a speed of 268.831 km/h (167.05 mph) behind a car used as a pacemaker, recording a time of 13.3 seconds for the distance of 1 km (0.62 miles), and 21.15 seconds for 1.60 km (1 mile). This record achieved in Bonneville Salt Lake, USA, on 3 October 1995.

## CYCLING UP STEPS

Hugues Richard from France pedalled up 1,600 stairs on a mountain bike at Montmartre, Paris within one hour on 5 October 2000.

The fastest ascent of the 747 stairs to the second platform of the Eiffel Tower, Paris, France, is held by

Hugues Richard with a time of 19 minutes, 4 seconds, which was recorded on 18 April 2002. He also has the record for the fastest descent with a time of 36 minutes, 26 seconds, achieved in 1998.

## DECATHLON

A record for the 24 x 1-hour decathlon was established by LG Freiberg/Neckar (Germany) on 3–4 July 1993. Each of the 24 athletes had to perform a decathlon within an hour, and the final aggregate result was 104,098 points.

## EGG AND SPOON – 4 X 100 RELAY

During the second Alternative Olympics held at the Costello International Sports Stadium, Hull, UK, on 12 June 1988 in front of a crowd of 3,000 spectators, a world record of 2 minutes, 02.17 seconds was recorded for the fastest 4 x 100-m egg and spoon relay. This was achieved by the Hull University Noddies team.

## EGG AND SPOON RACING

Josef Bohman, of Czechoslovakia, established the world record for egg and spoon racing over the distance of 50 m (164 ft) with a time of 7.9 seconds.

The most participants to take part in an egg and

spoon race, and who passed the finishing line with their egg intact and still on the spoon is 859, beating the previous record of 694. On 24 October 2003, 1,000 students at Raynes Park High School in south west London, UK, picked up their eggs and spoons and 'scrambled' 100 m (328 ft) in the world record attempt. Students were disqualified if they dropped their egg, or failed to cross the finishing line.

## FIGURE SKATING – LONGEST PIROUETTE

Nathalie Krieg, of Switzerland, holds the record for the longest pirouette. For a television show in Erfurt, Germany, on 11 October 1992, Nathalie set a record with a time of 3 minutes, 32 seconds for the longest pirouette. She said afterwards that she stopped the record attempt early because she had become afraid that it would become too boring for the television viewers.

## FLIGHT BY A MUSCLE POWERED AEROPLANE

Kanellos Kanellopoulos, of Greece, flew on 23 April 1988 with his muscle-powered aeroplane Daedalus from Heraklion, Crete, to the Island of Santorini, a distance of 119 km (74 miles) in a time of 3 hours, 53 minutes, 13 seconds.

## FLIGHT BY A MUSCLE POWERED HELICOPTER

In 1994, scientists from Japan constructed a helicopter, powered only by muscle, which managed to maintain flight for 19.46 seconds at a minimum height of 60 cm (23.6 in).

Since 1980, the American Helicopter Society (AHS) intends to reward, through the Igor Skilorsky Competition, the first team capable of meeting the following requirements. The team must design and build a helicopter that can hover for one minute while maintaining flight within a 10 m (32.8 ft) square and momentarily exceed the height of 3 m (9.84 ft). Furthermore, the machine must be powered exclusively by man force during the entire flight. The first team to fulfil these conditions under the supervision of the AHS, the National Aeronautic Association (NAA) and the Federation Aeronautique Internationale (FAI) will receive a prize of $20,000. The prize is still unclaimed. (Text quoted from a web site.)

## FOOTBALL CATCHING

The only person ever known to catch a football using the back of his hand is Dean Gould, of Felixstowe, UK. At the Brackenbury Sports Centre,

Felixstowe during December 2000, a football was kicked a measured distance of 23.8 m (78 ft 10 in) by Dave Robinson, also from Felixstowe, and was caught cleanly from the air.

## FOOTBALL – FASTEST ACCURATE SHOT

The fastest and most accurate kick of a football was measured using a police speed gun on 30 July 2001 at the Brackenbury Sports Centre, Felixstowe, Suffolk, UK. Dave Robinson, of Felixstowe, Suffolk, kicked a standard size-5 football into a five-a-side goal at a speed of 115.8 km/h (72 mph) from the penalty spot.

## FOOTBALL GROUND FUN RUN

Terry Twining, a superfit corporal of The Adjutant General's Corp based in Northern Ireland, ran a distance of 966 km (600 miles) to visit every Premiership football ground in England. Starting on 22 August 2002, the 29-year-old set off from Newcastle's St. James' Park ground, running a distance of 45 km (28 miles) every day for three weeks, visiting all 20 football clubs, culminating at Southampton's St. Mary's ground – just in time to watch their match against Everton.

# FOOTBALL JUGGLING

*Football (soccer ball) control, male:* Nikolai Kutsenko
(the Ukraine) juggled a regulation soccer ball for
24 hours, 30 minutes non-stop using feet, legs and
head, without the ball ever touching the ground
on 6 December 1995 at Kiev.

*Football (soccer ball) control, female:* Milene
Domingues (Brazil) juggled a football 55,187 times
in 9 hours, 6 seconds, in 1997.

*Walking while heading a soccer ball:* Agim Agushi
(Kosovo) covered 15.356 km (9 miles, 857 yd) in 3
hours, 12 minutes, 39 seconds on 27 October 2002
in Munich, Germany.

*Running marathon while keeping up a soccer ball:*
Dr Jan Skorkovský (Czech Repbublic) covered
42.195 km
(26 miles 385 yd) for the Prague City Marathon on
8 July 1990 in 7 hours, 18 minutes, 55 seconds.

*Running 100 m while juggling a soccer ball:* Manfred
Wagner (Switzerland): 15.9 seconds on 14 July 1996
at the 2nd Rekord-Klub Saxonia record festival in
Flensburg, Germany.

*Running 200 m while juggling a soccer ball:* Abraham Munoz (USA) in a record time of 40.26 seconds on 29 October 2000 in Wheaton College, Illinois, USA.

*Running 1,000 m while juggling a soccer ball:* Josef Lochman (Czechoslovakia): 5:03 minutes in 1986 in Valašské Meziříčí, Czechoslovakia.

*Running for 1 hour while juggling a soccer ball:* Josef Lochman (Czechoslovakia): 8,680 m (5 miles, 693 yds) in 1986 in Valašské Meziříčí, Czechoslovakia.

*Speed juggling, female record:* Tasha-Nicole Terani (USA) managed 137 touches (kicks) of a football in 30 seconds on 27 August 2003 in New York. She also holds the record for speed juggling in 60 seconds, beating the previous record of 262 on 4 September 2003 in Atlanta with 269 touches.

In 2002, Kurt Rothenfluh (Switzerland) demonstrated speed juggling for 2 minutes in a TV show. He was officially measured with 615 touches in 2 minutes, but the counting method was not accurate. However, the supposed correct result (about 570) would still surpass the records mentioned above.

*Heading a soccer ball, doubles passing:* Agim Agushi

and Bujar Ajeti (Kosovo) juggled a football between themselves 11,111 times in a time of 3 hours, 55 minutes, 20 seconds on 9 November 2003 in Stamberg, Germany.

*Heading a soccer ball, 30-second speed record:* Jacek Roszkowski (Poland) headed a football 173 times consecutively, on 23 July 1993 in Gdansk, Poland.

*Running up and down stairs while juggling a soccer ball (using feet and head):* Abraham Munoz (USA) climbed 2,754 steps walking upstairs as well as downstairs in 1:19 hours on 28 December 2002 in Morelia Michoacan, Mexico.

*Running up and down stairs while heading a soccer ball:* Agim Agushi (Kosovo) achieved this record by taking 1,920 steps walking upstairs, and 1,860 steps walking downstairs in a time of 1 hour, 12 minutes, 41 seconds on 2 August 2002 in the PTK Building in Prishtina, Kosovo.

## FOOTBALL REFEREE MARATHON

Vinko Jankovic, of Yugoslavia, set the record in 1983 when he acted as the referee in a soccer match between fans of Red Star Belgrad and Partizan

Belgrad. The match lasted 40 hours, and Vinko acted as a referee for the first half (20 hours).

## GOLF
The most holes played within 12 hours is 276 by Phillip Queller from the USA. Played at the Sky Links Golf Course, Riverside, California, USA, on 4 June 2001, Queller played without the use of any golf carts, or help of any kind. During the 12 hours, he made a total of 1,141 strokes, played 15 rounds and 6 holes, covering over 48.2 km (30 miles) of play and scoring a 17.4 average over par per round. He lost 5 golf balls during the day and wore out 8 pairs of golf gloves.

## HUMAN GRAND NATIONAL
The fastest recorded time in which a human has covered the entire 7.20-km (4.5-mile) Grand National course (without the aid of a horse) at Aintree is 40 minutes. This was achieved by Peter Regan, headmaster of St Michael's Junior School, Kirkby, Merseyside, UK, on 10 April 1983.

## ICE HOCKEY LEAGUE
East Germany had an ice hockey league with just two teams competing for the national championship each year.

## JOGA NIDRASANA

Roger Lussi, of Switzerland, performed the joga position Joga Nidrasana for a record time of 30:22 minutes.

## LEAPFROGGING

On 19 July 1974, Mike Barwell and Wally Adams, of East Yorkshire, UK, leapfrogged a distance of 27.4 km (17 miles 342 yd) in the permitted 8-hour period, averaging one leap every five yards, along the disused railway line between Sutton and Hornsea, Humberside, UK.

## MARATHON RUNNING – WHILE WEARING A DIVING SUIT

Lloyd Scott, of Rainham, Essex, UK, completed the London Marathon in the slowest time ever while wearing a rubberised canvas diving suit, including diving helmet, weighing 60 kg (132.2 lb). British charity fundraiser Lloyd took 5 days, 8 hours, 29 minutes, 46 seconds to complete the 42.195-km (26 mile 385 yd) course, raising over £100,000 for the charity Cancer and Leukaemia in Childhood.

## MATCHSTICK THROWING

The furthest a matchstick has been thrown, without wind assistance, is 34 m (111 ft), achieved by German Uwe Hohn. Not new to the record books, he holds the world record for spear (javelin) throwing. After his world record of 104.80 m (343.8 ft) in 1984, the dimensions of the javelin had to be changed due to the danger posed to spectators. With the changes to the javelin, this gave an opportunity to less muscled athletes such as the Czech Republic's Jan Zelezny to dominate the sport.

## MEDICINE BALL – CHEST PASSES

The following records are for the most passes of a 3.5-kg (7.7-lb) medicine ball from the chest to one person from another, and were set on 17 February 2004 at Felixstowe Leisure Centre, Felixstowe, UK.

*5 minutes* – 524 times, achieved by David Robinson and Paul Norris.

*1 minute* – 112 times, achieved by Richard Talbot and David Robinson.

*1 minute*, mixed – 92 times, achieved by Richard Talbot and Vanessa Relph.

## MEXICAN WAVE – LONGEST (MEASURED BY TIME, NOT DISTANCE)

On 16 May 1992, fans of the football team Werder Bremen, of Germany, celebrated the win of their team by conducting a Mexican wave lasting 22 minutes, 20 seconds and 22,100 fans were involved.

## MOTORCYCLING, LONG-DISTANCE

Between 11 May and 22 June 2002, Kevin Sanders and his wife, Julia (as passenger), circumnavigated the world on a motorcycle, a distance of 31,319 km (19,461 miles) in a time of 19 days, 8 hours, 25 minutes.

The husband and wife team also hold the Trans-Americas record (Alaska–Ushuaia). Starting at Deadhorse, Prudhoe Bay in Alaska, USA, they travelled a distance of 27,358 km (17,000 miles) in 35 days to finish in Ushuaia, Tierra del Fuego, Argentina.

## PARACHUTE JUMPS

Jay Stokes, 47, of Yuma, Arizona, USA, broke the world record for the most consecutive parachute jumps in a 24-hour period. On 12 November 2003, Stokes completed the record attempt with 534 parachute jumps, beating the previous record of 500 held by fellow American Michael Zang. Each jump was done from 6,400 m (21,000 ft) above ground and averaged two minutes, 41 seconds per jump. He used 22 parachutes and two airplanes for the jumps.

## PEDAL BOATING

On 18 August 2000, British adventurer Jason Lewis, 32, of Bridgeport, Dorset, UK, became the first person to complete the 11,265-km (7,000-mile) crossing of the Pacific Ocean from the USA to Australia in *Mokasha*, a 7.90-m (26-ft) human-powered pedal boat. With Lewis was April Abril, a teacher from Rye, Colorado, USA, who helped pedal the raft into Port Douglas, Queensland. She was one of three friends who took turns helping him on island-hopping legs across the ocean.

## PENNY-FARTHING CYCLE RIDING

The record for the furthest distance travelled in 24 hours on a penny-farthing cycle belongs to Manfred Cizek (Austria). A distance of 546 km (339 miles) was recorded during a race in Schötz, Switzerland. The cycle used was an 1885 bicycle replica.

Steve Stevens broke the record for riding a penny-farthing across the US on 24 June 2000. Riding an 1887 Rudge 54' penny-farthing 'ordinary' high wheel bike, he travelled 5,230 km (3,250 miles), and his total journey, from San Francisco to Boston took 29 days, 9 hours 3 minutes, beating the previous record of 34 days.

## PENNY-FARTHING SPEED RECORDS

Vladimir Kotik (Czech Republic) rode a distance of 50 m (164 ft) in 5.07 seconds and 1,000 m in 1 minute, 58.02 seconds. Both records were set on 20 May 1997.

Matthias Konder (Trier, Germany) rode a distance of 2,000 m (6561.7 ft) in 4 minutes, 14.1 seconds on 14 September 1984 in Faak am See, Austria.

## POLE CLIMBING

The World Pole Climbing Association sanctions the records under this category, and world records can only be set at WPA-recognised events with electronic timing equipment.

The record time for climbing a 24.4-m (80-ft) pole is 10.58 seconds, achieved by Mark Bryden (Australia).

The women's record for climbing a 24.4-m (80-ft) pole is 21.06 seconds, set in 1999 at Eurodisney, Paris, France, by Aida Mauricio (France).

## PUSHUPS

*Most pushups by one person over the course of a year:* 1,500,230, between 21 October 1988 and 1 October 1989 by Paddy Doyle, of Birmingham, UK.

*Most one-arm pushups in one week:* 16,723 also by Paddy.

*Most one-arm pushups achieved in 5 minutes:* 546 by Doug Pruden on 30 July 2003, set in Edmonton Alberta, Canada. On the same occasion, Doug broke the record for 30 minutes with 1,382 one-arm pushups.

*Most one-arm pushups achieved in 10 minutes:* 441 by Giuseppe Cusano (UK) on 24 November 2003 during the Fulham versus Portsmouth football match held at Loftus Road football stadium.

*Most pushups done on fresh hen's eggs:* 112, performed by Johann Schneider of Austria.

On 9 July 2003, Doug Pruden completed 1,000 pushups on his fists in the time of 18 minutes, 13 seconds, set in Edmonton, Alberta, Canada.

The female speed record for pushups belongs to Renata Hamplová from the Czech Republic. She completed 426 full pushups in 10 minutes, and 190 in 3 minutes.

## ROLLER CYCLING, FASTEST
The highest speed registered by a man roller cycling was achieved by Manfred Nüscheler (Switzerland) in Bern with a recorded speed of 164.1 km/h (101.97 mph). He also holds the distance records for 500 m (1640 ft) with a time of 14.36 seconds, and 1,000 m (3,281 ft) with a time of 32.48 seconds.

## ROPE SKIPPING – 2, 3 AND 6 HOURS
Dr Jan Skorkovský, of Czech Republic, skipped 23,344 times in 2 hours and 33,956 times in 3 hours (both 1986 in Prague). In 1985, he skipped 60,300 times within 6 hours.

## ROPE SKIPPING – 24-HOUR RECORDS
On 26 March 2004, sportsman Jimmy Payne, of Waterford City, Republic of Ireland, smashed the existing solo 24-hour skipping record of 130,000 when he skipped an amazing 141,221 skips in a 24-hour period. In front of a huge crowd at the City Square Shopping Centre, Payne – a holder of four national boxing titles – skipped an average 175–180 skips per minute, using the record attempt to raise

more than £26,000 for the Our Lady's Hospital for Sick Children charity.

Far from being new to record breaking, Jimmy Payne was the leader of the team that set the 24-hour team skipping record of 244,949 skips in 2002, a record which he aims to beat sometime during 2004.

## ROPE SKIPPING

The longest distance travelled rope skipping is 2,034 km (1,264 miles). This record was achieved in 1963 by Tom Morris, 71, of Australia, who skipped from Brisbane to Cairns.

Carlos Argueta (Columbia) skipped the Los Angeles Marathon on 5 March 1995 in a world record time of 5 hours, 19 minutes, 14 seconds.

Lucie Kvasničkova (Czech Republic) set a record for rope-skipping while running 50 m in 9.3 seconds.

## RUNNING – 1,500 M

The oldest man to have run the 1,500 m is Les Amey from Brisbane, Australia. At 101, Mr Amey won the 100-years-and-over category at the World Veterans Games in Brisbane on 13 July 2001 in a time of 19 minutes, 59 seconds.

## RUNNING – BACKPACK WITH WEIGHT

Multi-record breaker Paddy Doyle, of Erdington, Birmingham, UK, holds a number of stamina records, but none more impressive than the records he has accumulated for running with a backpack full of weights. His records include:

1 mile with 18.1 kg (40 lb): 5:35 minutes, on 7 March 1993, in Bally Cotton, Ireland.
5 miles with 25.40 kg (56 lb): 36:49 minutes, on 9 May 1999, Stoneheigh Park, Coventry, UK.
10 miles with 18.1 kg (40 lb): 1:24 hrs, on 7 March 1993, Bally Cotton, Ireland.
London Marathon with 19.96 kg (44 lb): 4:42 hours, on 21 April 1991.

The fastest time a marathon has been run while carrying a 22.68-kg (50lb) backpack is 5 hours, 4 minutes. Paddy Doyle completed this athletic feat at the London Marathon on 12 April 1992.

## RUNNING – MASS RELAYS

If a relay is not marked as 'women', men and women can run. A runner must not run more than once. In each case, a baton must be used.

*100 X 4 M: RUNNERS FROM ERFURT*

*(GERMANY):* 2:24.7 min, Erfurt (8 April 1986).

*50 X 50 M:* SKV Eglosheim (Germany) 5:19.9 min (29 September 2001).

*100 X 100 M:* Chummen Sport (Switzerland): 18:36,88 min. (26 August 2001).

*100 X 100 M (WOMEN):* junior runners from Baden-Württemberg (Germany): 21:16.99 min, Stuttgart (1 JULY 2001).

*1,000 X 100 M:* TUS Freiberg, (Germany): 4:08:29,6 hrs, Freiberg/Neckar (17 July 1999).

*100 X 1,000 M:* Technical University of Charkov (USSR): 4:42:25 hrs, Charkov (May 1985).

*100 X 1,000 M (WOMEN):* Institut für Lehrerbildung Berlin (German Democratic Republic): 6:43:38 hrs, Berlin (1986).

## RUNNING – CUSTARD-FILLED WELLIES

The world record for running 100 m while wearing custard-filled wellies was achieved at the Alternative Olympics held at the Costello International Sports Stadium, Hull, UK, on 12 June 1988 by Pete Allison with a time of 13.79 seconds.

The fastest female in custard-filled wellies over 100 m is Sally Lowe of Hassocks, West Sussex, UK, with a time of 16.01 seconds.

The fastest mile for a veteran (over 50) is 5

minutes, 21.37 seconds by Derek Earl, 52, of Hassocks, West Sussex, UK. Both the above records were set at the Costello Sports Stadium, Hull, Humberside, UK, on 31 August 1986.

The fastest female over 1 mile is Barbara Rickard of Ditchling, West Sussex, UK, with a time of 8 minutes, 14.80 seconds set at Adastra Park, Hassocks, West Sussex, UK, on 1 September 1984.

On 17 May 1986, the 'Brentwood Police & Gateway International Custard-Filled Welly Challengers' consisting of 27 sticky-legged individuals, successfully completed a 42.19-km (26 mile 385 yd) relay marathon in the record time of 3 hours, 3 minutes, 26.6 seconds at the High School, Shenfield, Essex, UK.

Not to be outdone, the ladies came along and triumphed also, recording a world-beating time of 4 hours, 50 minutes, 16.41 seconds for the same distance.

## RUNNING – THREE-LEGGED RACING

On 6 April 1986, Dirk Lübeck and Thomas Raabe, of East Berlin, Germany, set a three-legged racing record over the distance of 50 m in a time of 6.6 seconds at a sporting event held in Berlin. On the same occasion, Sabine Roos and Gritta Zölfel (also from East Berlin) established the women's record with a time of 8 seconds.

Olympian Harry Hillman and Lawson Robertson, both from the USA, hold the record for running the three-legged 91.40 m (100 yards) distance race in a time of 11.0 seconds in New York on 24 April 1909. Harry Hillman won three gold medals at the 1904 Olympics held in St Louis, USA, which included 400 m, 200 m hurdles, and 400 m hurdles.

In 1984, Czechoslovakians Emanuel Cerny and Josef Bohman, set the world record for three-legged racing over the distance of 400 m with a time of 1:22:2 minutes.

## RUNNING – UNDERWATER MARATHON

The first underwater marathon ever 'run' was achieved on 29–30 June 2003 by Wolfgang Kuhlow (Germany), who set the record of 24 hours, 24 minutes, 47 seconds in a swimming pool in Lehnsahn, Germany while having to carry 40 kg (88.18 lb) of lead weights. In 2004, Wolfgang Kuhlow ran another underwater marathon, beating his own record with a time of 22 hours.

The record for 'running' the fastest underwater marathon in a natural lake (which is much more difficult!) goes to Lloyd Scott from Essex, UK, who 'ran' the marathon 10 m (33 ft) below the surface of Loch Ness in Scotland while wearing a 60-year-old diving suit weighing 86 kg (190 lb), and weighted diving boots during September and October 2003. Organised as a fundraiser, it took Lloyd 12 days (including breaks), however the total time for the marathon was 5 days, 8 hours, 29 minutes, 46 seconds. He collected money for the Children with Leukaemia Children's Marathon Challenge.

## RUNNING WAITER

The fastest running waiter in the world is Roger Bourbon from Canada. The record requires the runner to be dressed in waiter's clothing, and carrying a bottle and a glass. The bottle may not be touched, and no liquid may be spilled. Roger holds the following records:

1,000 m in 2 minutes, 59 seconds, on 4 December 1983 in Beverly Hills, California, USA.

5,000 m in 17minutes, 44 seconds, on 5 December 1982 in Beverly Hills, California, USA.

10,000 m in 36 minutes, 56 seconds, on 9 December 1979 in Beverly Hills, California, USA.

20,000 m in 1 hour, 14 minutes and 58 seconds on 18 October 1981, set in Paris, France.

Marathon in 2 hours, 47 minutes on 9 May 1982 in London, UK.

## SCOOTER RIDING
The furthest distance covered in 24 hours of scooter riding is 329.156 km (204.54 miles), by Miroslav Frais (Czechoslovakia) at Ostrava from 31 May 1979 to 01 June 1979.

The fastest time recorded for scooter riding over the distance of 100 km (62 miles) is 4 hours, 30 seconds, achieved by Harald Hel of Austria. He also holds the record for the fastest time for scooter riding over the distance of 200 km (124 miles) with a time of 10 hours, 40 minutes. Both records were on the street, using adult's scooters.

## SCUBA DIVING
A record number of six scuba divers were able to stay underwater for one hour using only one bottle of oxygen. This record was established in Pelhrimov, Czech Republic, on 16 December 1995.

## SHOOTING
Ad Topperwein was, without doubt, the greatest marksman of his time and, in all probability, the best trick shot gunman the world has ever known. In

December 1907 at the Old San Antonio Exposition and Fair Grounds, Texas, USA, and using three .22 calibre rifles, Topperwein shot seven hours a day for ten consecutive days at 72,500 5.7-cm (2¼-in) diameter wooden blocks, each pitched to a height of 7.5–9 m (25–30 ft) from a distance of 7.5 m (25 ft). Ad had 60,000 blocks made, and his last 22,500 shots were at pieces of the original blocks. In the ten days, Topperwein missed just nine times.

## SHOPPING-TROLLEY RUN
The rules for this category are quite simple: a rolling shopping trolley has to be pushed for one hour by one team member. The second team member has a much easier job; he or she sits in the shopping trolley. The world record is 12,660 m (41535 ft) by Císař and Pavel Petroušek (Czech Republic) in 1996.

## SIT-UPS
Paddy Doyle, of Erdington, Birmingham, UK, completed 5,000 sit-ups with a 22.68-kg (50-lb) weight in a time of 5 hours on 22 August 1988 at The Firebird, Birmingham, UK.

## SKIING – 100 X 1000 M RELAY

Sports students from SC DHfK Leipzig (Germany) completed a 100 x 1000 m skiing relay in 7 hours, 6 minutes, 36 seconds on 19 January 1989 in Schneckenstein, Germany.

## SKIING – MARATHON, SIX ON ONE SKI

A team of 6 from Switzerland completed the marathon distance (42.195 km [26 miles 385 yd]) from Maloja to Zuoz (Switzerland) in a time of 4 hours. 39 minutes, 30 seconds on 11 March 1990. The six skied the distance on a single 8.07 m-long (26.5-ft-long) ski.

## SNOOKER

The highest possible break at snooker is not, as commonly believed, 147. By adhering rigorously to the rules a break of 155 is possible. In order for this to happen, one player must play a foul stroke and render his opponent snookered. The referee will then call a 'free ball' and the snookered player may now attempt to pot ANY ball on the table. If potted, this ball has the value of a red (one point) and is re-spotted; then the player may continue with a colour. Thus, by sequence, a break of 155 is possible. It was reported in March 1980 that Alex

'Hurricane' Higgins had achieved a break of 154 in just such a fashion.

## SOCCER BALL BALANCING

*ON THE FOOT*
Abraham Munoz, of USA, balanced a regulation-size football on his foot for 13 minutes, 36 seconds on 3 August 2001 in Carpentersville, Illinois, USA.

*ON THE HEAD*
Adalberto Sanchez, of Mexico, balanced a regulation-size football on his head for 2 hours, on 21 December 2002 in Morelia Michoacan, Mexico.

## SQUATS
Kevin Z. Molnar, Hungarian Olympic weightlifter, set a new world record of squatting in Berlin, Germany by doing 170 repetitions with 100 kg (220 lb) at a bodyweight of 74.8 kg (165 lb). The previous record of 138 repetitions was held by a 99.8-kg (220-lb) lifter, so to be able to lift more reps and be 24.9 kg (55 lb) lighter is an amazing feat of strength and endurance.

## SQUAT THRUSTS

The highest number of squat thrusts performed in one week is 21,347. Paddy Doyle from Erdington, Birmingham, UK, set the record during May 1998 at the Living Well Gym in Solihull, UK.

On 12 August 1995, Paddy Doyle set the world record for the most squat thrusts in 30 minutes when he performed 1,360 at the Moseley Arms Public House, Birmingham, UK.

## STADIUM SINGING – BY FANS

The longest sing along by sports fans in a stadium is 85 minutes. This record requires a minimum of 2,500 fans singing without a break. Fans of the ice hockey club ETC Grimmitschau achieved this record on 6 January 1999. Their team won against ESV Bayreuth (3–2).

## STAIR CLIMBING

Vimochan Beauvais (France) started on 22 June 2000 to climb up and down the 222 stairs to Montmatre in Paris. For 17 hours a day, he climbed up and down the stairs – 161 times per day until he reached his goal of climbing 2,000,000 steps. Vimochen Beauvais's record-breaking career started in 1982 when he climbed 100,000 stairs, followed by 200,000 in 1984, 250,000 in 1990 and 1,000,000 in 1991.

## SWIMMING WITH HANDS AND FEET TIED

In 1935, Tom Morris set a world record for swimming a distance of yards 45.7 m (50 yd) in 1 minute, 6 seconds, while his hands and feet were tied, in Bendigo, Australia. He also swam 91.40 m (100 yd) in the same fashion in a time of 2 minutes, 22.2 seconds in 1928, in Sydney, Australia, and 182.88 m (200 yd) in 8 minutes, 15 seconds in 1964, in Mackay, Australia.

Henry Kuprash Vili, a Georgian historian, swam the Dardanelles from Europe to Asia with his hands and feet bound tightly at four places. He swam the 12-km (7.40-mile) distance in 3 hours, 15 minutes on 30 August 2002.

## SWIMMING – HIGH ALTITUDE DISTANCE

On 3 August 2002, Chinese physical education teacher Zhang Jian, 38, swam 34.2 km (21.20 miles) across the Fuxianhu Lake in South Western China's Yunnan province in 12 hours, 1 minute. The high altitude lake is approximately 1,800 m (5,905 ft) above sea level. With the water averaging 87 m (285 ft) in depth and 158 m (518 ft) at the deepest measurement, it is the second deepest fresh-water lake in China.

## SWIMMING – LONGEST DISTANCE

Slovenian Martin Strel, 48, completed the longest distance ever swam in 68 days when he covered the entire 3,862-km (2,400-mile) length of America's Mississippi River. Starting in Minnesota and swimming for 12 hours a day, Strel broke his own world record of 3,003 km (1,866 miles), a record he had previously set when he swam the Danube River, and arrived at the Gulf of Mexico.

## SWIMMING DOG – FASTEST

Umbra, a mixed breed dog, part Labrador and part Greyhound, was born in 1990, and found as a stray by former American swimmer Ted Erikson. She began swimming tandem with Erikson in Lake Michigan, USA, during the summer of 1991, establishing a benchmark time of 32 minutes for a mile. The following years, Umbra decreased her mile time to 28.5 minutes. Since then, she has accumulated a number of swimming records for the fastest dog, including:

A round trip of the Peace River crossing in Port Charlotte, Florida, USA, on 3 September

1994, a distance of 3.86 km (2.4 miles) in a time of 65 minutes.

An open water Lake Michigan swim in Chicago, Illinois, USA, on 7 October 1994 – a distance of 4.34 km (2.7 miles) in 72 minutes.

The Bosporus crossing (Asia to Europe) in Turkey on 22 July 1995 – a distance of 3.20 km(2 miles) in a time of 31 minutes.

The Big Shoulders Masters Lake Swim in Chicago, Illinois, USA, on 9 August 1986 – a distance of 5 km (3.1 miles) in 77 minutes.

## SWIMMING, MASS RELAY

The record for a 1000 x 50 m freestyle swimming relay is 7 hours, 31 minutes, 45 seconds, by SC Einheit Dresden (East Germany), on 13 July 1988.

## SYNCHRONISED WEIGHT LIFTING

The rules for this record are that two weight lifters have to lift the weight on a bar simultaneously.

Manfred Nerlinger and Ronny Weller (both from Germany) lifted 330 kg (728 lb) on 1 February 1997 in Wiesbaden, Germany.

## TABLE TENNIS – SOLO BALL HITTING

On 3 June 2002, David Downes Junior, from Felixstowe, Suffolk, UK set the record for hitting a table tennis ball between bats held in both left and right hands when he hit the ball 119 times in a time of 1 minute.

## TEARING PLAYING CARDS

On 15 March 1930, Milo Barus (real name: Emil Bahr), of Germany, tore a deck of 135 playing cards in Paris at a 'World's Strongest Man' contest.

## TENNIS – LONGEST RALLY

The world's longest rally took place on 5 February 2000 at the Rancho Valencia Resort in Rancho Santa Fe near San Diego, USA between Ray Miller and his friend Rob Peterson. Miller and Peterson, who both live in Ukiah, Oregon, USA, hit 15,674 shots in 9 hours, 45 minutes, beating the previous record of 15,464, set by Will Duggan and Ron Kapp.

On 26 September 1999, Rob Peterson and Ray Miller set the record for the longest rally keeping two tennis balls in play. Both players hit a total of 2,789 shots from the baseline for over 35 minutes.

Rob Peterson also holds the record for the most serves hit over the longest period of time. Set on 5 December 1998, Peterson hit an amazing 8,017 serves.

## TENNIS BALL BOUNCING

The most number of bounces recorded of a tennis ball on the edge of a tennis racquet in 1 minute is 215, by Dean Gould, of Felixstowe, Suffolk, UK, during a show held at the offices of Magnum Spedition, Felixstowe in June 1999.

## THROW, FURTHEST

The furthest throw of an item with an unaided arm is 406 m (1,333 ft). Erin Hemming, 26, from Mendocino, California, USA, accomplished this unwieldy feat on 14 July 2003 at the Golden Gate National Recreation Centre near Fort Funston, San Francisco, USA, when he threw an Aerobie Pro flying ring further than anyone has ever thrown any object in the history of measurement. The distance was measured four times with a Leica Laser Rangefinder.

## TRAIN PULLING WITH TEETH – WHILE WALKING ON HANDS

Jan Knotek (Czech Republic) pulled a railway wagon weighing 15 tons for a distance of 1.40 m while walking on hands and pulling the rope using only his teeth.

## TRAMPOLINE-TO-TRAMPOLINE SOMERSAULT

Ukrainian somersault champion Andrey Bezruchenko, a 36-year-old father of one, broke his own world record for bouncing and spinning between two trampolines, when he covered the distance of 4.62 m (15.10 ft), smashing his previous best of 4.52 m (14.80 ft). Bezruchenko, a performer with the Moscow State Circus, broke the record during a circus visit in the grounds of Cardiff Castle in Wales, UK, on 14 April 2003.

## TREADMILL RUNNING

Organised by the extreme sports web site 'extrem.hu', Edit Berces (Hungary) ran 247.2 km (153.60 miles) on a treadmill on 8–9 March 2004 in Budapest. She not only beat the female record of 181.3 km (112.66 miles) set exactly two days before by Christine Sextl (Germany), but also the male record by Serge Arbona (USA) who ran 245.05 km (152.27 miles) on 24–25 January 2004. En route, Edit broke the record for 100 miles (14:15:08 hrs), once again breaking Serge Arbona's male record (14:22:49 hours).

A new male record was set by Christopher Bergland (USA) on 29–30 April 2004 at the Kiehl's flagship store in New York. Christopher ran 247.45 km (153.76 miles) within 24 hours.

## OTHER TREADMILL RECORDS

The 12-hour record belongs to Serge Arbona with 137.89 km (85.68 miles).

The 48-hour record for running on a treadmill belongs to Tony Mangan (Ireland), who ran 372.06 km (231.2 miles) on 25–26 October 2003 in Dublin.

Ultra-runner David Taylor from Australia recorded the longest distance run on a treadmill in 7 days. David started the run on 26 November 2003, clocking a distance of 455.83 km (283.2 miles) when he finished the challenge on 3 December 2003 – the equivalent to a marathon-and-a-half every day.

The fastest treadmill marathon was completed by Josh Cox (USA) with 2 hours, 31 minutes, 4 seconds at Boston Marathon Expo, 17 April 2004.

The record for running 100-km (62 miles) goes to Richard Fröhlich, of Vogt, Germany. He ran this distance on a treadmill in 7 hours, 46 minutes, 26 seconds.

Martin Pröll (Austria) set a world record time of 7 minutes, 53 seconds for running a distance of 3,000 m on a treadmill on 17 January 2003 in Wels, Austria.

## UNDERWATER WALKING

The record for walking 50 m in a swimming pool while another person is standing (balanced) on that person's shoulders goes to Romy Meinecke (balancing Frank Jucht) both from Zwickau, Germany, in a record time of 59 seconds. The head of the walking person has to be completely underwater all of the time.

The longest underwater walk was performed by five Australians from 2 to 4 September 1983. They walked a distance of 82.9 km (271,982 ft) along the bottom of Sydney Harbour.

## UNICYCLING

Stefan Gauler, of Switzerland, travelled a distance of 21.290 km (13.23 miles) in one hour on 24 September 2000 at the Saxonia Record Festival, Bregenz, Austria.

The Rev. Lars J Clausen, who left a job as campus minister at East Lansing's University Lutheran Church in 2001, broke the world distance record for riding a unicycle when he rode for 205 days, a distance of 14,703 km (9,136 miles). Beginning on 22 April 2002 at the shore of the Pacific Ocean in Neah Bay, Washington, USA, he followed a route that took him through many states, ending on 12 November 2002.

The unicycle rider 'Wobbling' Wally Watts was reported to have ridden 19,300 km (11,993 miles) around the world.

## UNICYCLE SKIPPING

The most rope jumps in one minute while on a unicycle is 209 skips. Amy Shields, 11, of St Paul, Minnesota, USA, broke the previous record of 169 on 23 February 2002.

The men's record is tied at 206 skips, set by Brady Witbeck and Ryan Woessner, both from Mounds View, Minnesota.

## WALKING LUNGES

The record for the fastest mile walked while 'lunging' was broken on 9 November 2003 by Stephan Ehrenfelder (Austria) in Stamberg, Germany, with a time of 24 minutes, 15 seconds.

## WATER-FILLED WELLY WANGING

Often performed at alternative athletic events, the world record for water-filled welly wanging is held by Mel Brewer with a distance thrown of 15.42 m (50 ft 6 in).

## WEIGHT BALL JUGGLING

Milan Roskopf (Slovakia) juggled with three 7.25-kg (15.98-lb) weight balls for 52 seconds on 27 October 2002 at Neufahrn, Germany. He is also the record holder for juggling three 3-kg (6.6-lb) weight balls (7:07 minutes), 5 kg (11-lb) balls (1:35 min) and 8.5 kg (18.7-lb) balls (39.5 seconds). He ran 100 m in 24 seconds while juggling three 5 kg (11-lb) balls and completed the 1999 Bratislava – Heinburg half marathon while juggling three balls weighing 1 kg (2.2-lb) each.

## WHEELCHAIR – 24-HOUR DISTANCE

The greatest distance covered in 24 hours in a wheelchair is 234.556 km (145.75 miles). Set in 1990 by Friedhelm Hebel (Germany) in Basel, Switzerland.

## WHEELCHAIR DANCING

On 26 May 1993, five pairs of wheelchair dancers from RBG Dortmund, Germany, danced non-stop for 24 hours.

## WHEELCHAIR DANCE – MOST PARTICIPANTS

Performed by 46 members of the Beautiful Gate – Methodist Ministry for the Disabled, at Putra Stadium, Bukit Jalil, Malaysia, on 1 January 2000.

## WHEELCHAIR PUSHING

On Friday 8 September 2000, members, friends and supporters of Cumbria Cerebral Palsy Society's Maryport Branch, began their attempt at beating the world distance record for pushing a wheelchair in 24 hours. Using Whitehaven's Copeland Athletic Stadium, many of the participants were fell runners and road runners, and at 14:43 hours on Saturday 9 September 2000, the world record was broken with the distance of 387.975 km (241 miles 133 yd 2 ft 3 in).

## WHEELCHAIR WHEELIE

After setting out as a fundraiser for wheelchair ramps in his community, Robert M. Hensel of Oswego,

New York, USA, set the record for the longest long-distance wheelie in a wheelchair. On 3 October 2002, at the Pathfinder Sports Complex in Scriba, New York, USA, Robert Hensel went around the sports track in his wheelchair on two wheels continuously for more than 2 hours, covering a distance of 9.94 km (6.178 miles).

The speed record holder is Marián Timko (Czech Republic) who needed 28.25 seconds for a distance of 50 m on the two back wheels of his wheelchair on 10 June 2001.

**WIND SURFING**
The longest recorded time established for riding a wind surfing practice board on dry land is 12 hours, 39 minutes by Patrick Cardez at Cherbourg, France, on 15 May 1990.

# THE AMAZING ...
# PADDY DOYLE

*'What I have achieved has never been about
money or fame – I just love the challenge and
thrill of beating people ...'*
Paddy Doyle

Born and raised on the streets of Erdington in Birmingham, UK, a young Paddy Doyle did not know that one day he would break 125 Course, Regional, National, British, European and World Fitness endurance records in several different sporting disciplines. But the world endurance champion is the first to concede that it was a three-year stint in the Army that paved the way forward to the position he is in today.

In 1984, at the age of 21, Paddy left Birmingham for Aldershot and the 2nd Battalion, the Parachute regiment. He settled immediately into the disciplined lifestyle of soldiering and graduated from his training platoon as champion recruit. 'I just switched on and adapted my behaviour from day one,' he says. 'I wanted that red beret so much that I would have done anything. I felt that the Paras was an elite regiment and I wanted to be one of the best.'

In 1987, Paddy left the Army a stronger, better man. 'The Army sorted me out, made me more mature and gave me the kick up the backside I needed,' he said. 'It made me realise that I had the potential to make some money out of sport.'

It was in a market in Warwickshire that, by chance, Paddy stumbled across his true vocation. 'I picked up this tattered old copy of a book of

records, looked at the various press-ups records and thought, I can do better than that.'

Within three months he had set his first world endurance record. At a city centre venue in Birmingham, Paddy set out to achieve as many press-ups as possible in four-and-a-half hours – with a 22.68 kg (50 lb) steel plate on his back! When time ran out, he had achieved a staggering 4,100 – a rate of approximately 15 press-ups per minute.

'Things just escalated from there,' he says. 'Companies began offering me sponsorship and it became something of a full-time job.'

After 14 years, with 122 of the world's toughest strength, speed and stamina records to his name,

Paddy has decided to take early retirement. 'I've had a good run and I want to retire at the top while I've got no mental, dental or physical problems.'

He may be calling time on his extraordinary career, but one thing is certain: his competitive zeal will never diminish. 'What I have achieved has never been about money or fame – I just love the challenge and thrill of beating people.

'I don't mind if anyone reading this now goes out and takes one of my records, but I will say this to them: "Just because you beat one of them does not mean you have beaten Paddy Doyle – you've got to break all 122 records before you can claim that."'

## PADDY'S WORLD RECORDS INCLUDE:

### PUSHUPS
*with a 22.68-kg (50-lb) plate weight on his back:*
4,100, 28 May 1987, Calthorpe Old Boys
Birmingham, UK

*one-armed, one hour:* 2,521, 12 Feb 1996, Holly Lane
Sports Centre, Birmingham
*one year:* 1,500,230, 21 October 1988–1 October
1989, Holiday Inn Hotel, Birmingham, UK

## SIT-UPS

*with a 22.68-kg (50-lb) plate weight, 30 minutes:* 580, 7 March 1991, The Wrexham, Birmingham, UK

*with a 22.68-kg (50-lb) plate weight:* 5,000 in 5 hours, 28 August 1988, The Firebird, Birmingham, UK

## SQUAT THRUSTS

*in one week:* 21,347, May 1998. Living Well Gym, Solihull, UK

*in one hour:* 3,743, 4 May 1998, Staminas Gym, Birmingham, UK

## BURPEES

*in five hours:* 4,921, 25 November 1995, Dubliner Public House, Birmingham, UK

*in one week:* 21,309, July 1999, Fairford Air Show, Gloucester, UK

## BACK PACK RUNNING

*50 miles with an 18.14-kg (40-lb) weight:* 11 hours, 56 minutes, 22 seconds, 4 September 1993, Bally Cotton, Ireland

*Marathon with a 22.68-kg (50-lb) weight:* 5 hours, 4 minutes, 12 April 1992, London Marathon, UK

## CONTACT SPORTS

*Karate*: monthly sparring, 467 full contact rounds (in 23 days), September 1996, Holly Lane Sports Centre, Birmingham, UK

*Boxing*: weekly sparring, 203 rounds, 31 January–6 February 1995, Holly Lane Sports Centre, Birmingham, UK

## MISCELLANEOUS

*Weight Lifting:* One hour: 24,258.5 kg (53,480 lb), 9 November 1990, Fox Hollies Leisure Centre, Birmingham, UK

*Log Carrying:* 100 times on a distance of 7.62 m (25 ft) (log weighing 25.4 kg [56 lb]), 21 minutes, 40 seconds, 31 October 1994, Cannon Hill Park, Birmingham, UK

# THE AMAZING ...
# MAT HAND

*'... presenting world record-breaking attempts as Live Art invites the viewer to consider the underlying motivations for these events, our aspiration to achieve and the lengths to which we will go to be remembered ...'*
Mat Hand, December 2003

Like many of our record breakers, Mat Hand is an established world record breaker, though relatively new to the mainstream record-breaking circuit. Born and bred in Nottingham, 31-year-old Mat studied a Contemporary Arts Degree in 2001 at Nottingham Trent University before entering competitively into the world of the extraordinary. Unlike the other record breakers featured in this book, Mat performs his record-breaking attempts as dramatic Live Art staged in art galleries in Germany and the UK. 'By asking the audience to witness the event invites the viewer to consider the underlying motivations for these events and the complex human conditions which underpin this cultural phenomenon.'

The records which Mat is interested in are primarily human achievement records concerned with 'freakish dimensions, incredible feats of endurance and bizarre skills'. Quite simply, the type of records which are featured throughout this book.

On 9 May 2001, Mat performed his first world record attempt at a Waterstone's Bookshop Gallery in Nottingham. After taking over 4 hours and 129 attempts, Mat broke the world beer mat flipping record of 111 (held by fellow 'amazing' record breaker Dean Gould since 1993) when he flipped

and caught 112 beer mats, and thus beginning his record-breaking career.

Since then, Mat has achieved records for the longest table tennis rally, the tallest sugar cube tower and gastronomic records for eating peas and grapes.

When asked what motivates him, Mat says about record breaking, 'It is seen by many as an achievement that combines success and individuality through a heady mixture of competition, ambition and dedication. Record breaking offers an opportunity to prove that you are unique, an achiever, somebody special. You are not subsumed into a mass of producers or consumers. You stand alone.'

With his unique stance on record breaking, relative newcomer Mat Hand is a record-breaking performer who is considered by many – including us – to be a future 'great' in the record-breaking world, which qualifies him entry into *The Book of Alternative Records'* 'amazing …' hall of fame.

Unfazed by the attention or his motive for the way he performs his record-breaking attempts, Mat states, 'Presenting a world record-breaking attempt as Live Art invites the viewer to consider the underlying motivations for these events, our aspiration to achieve and the lengths to which we will go to be remembered.'

## MAT'S WORLD RECORDS INCLUDE:

### BEER MAT FLIPPING
Mat flipped a stack of beer mats balanced on the edge of a table 180 degrees and caught 112, at Waterstone's Bookshop, 9 May 2001.

### GRAPE EATING
3-minute record – using a plastic spoon, Mat devoured 133 grapes during a performance staged on 8 November 2001.

### PEA EATING
3-minute record – using a cocktail stick, Mat ate

211 peas during an art exhibition performed on 8
November 2001.

## TALLEST SUGAR CUBE TOWER

The tallest sugar cube tower measures 145.5 cm
(57.3 in) in height and was achieved during a
performance at an art gallery in Germany held
in 2003.

## LONGEST TABLE TENNIS RALLY

Mat Hand in collaboration with Leif Alexis broke
the longest table tennis rally record with a time of
5 hours, 8 minutes, 22 seconds.

# THE ARTS,
# ENTERTAINMENT
# AND PASTIMES

## BEER MAT FLIPPING

Mention the words 'beer mat' and Felixstowe man Dean Gould will really flip his lid. Dean holds virtually every beer mat flipping world record in this category.

Standardisation requires that the beer mats be approximately 10 cm sq (1.55 in sq). The mats must revolve half a turn after being flipped from the edge of a table before being caught in the same hand with the fingers on top, thumb underneath in a pincer position.

*SIMULTANEOUS (TWO HANDS) FLIPPING:* 130 (65 caught in each hand), January 1987, Feathers Public Inn, Walton, Felixstowe, UK.

*SPEED FLIPPING:* 1,000 mats flipped in 45 seconds (25 piles of 40), October 1993, BBC Television Centre, London, UK.

In addition, Dean holds the world record for beer mat catching. In July 2000 at the Brackenbury Sports Centre, Felixstowe, UK, Dean caught 2,390 beer mats flipped from the elbow (similar to coin snatching) in one hand, palm uppermost.

Until recently, Dean held the record for right-hand flipping with 111 mats flipped 180°, January 1993, Edinburgh, UK. However, aptly named Mat Hand, of Nottingham, UK, flipped a stack of beer mats balanced on the edge of a table 180° and caught 112 on 9 May 2001, during a publicity event held at Waterstone's Bookshop Gallery, in Nottingham, UK. It took over 4 hours and 129 attempts to beat the previous long-time record of 111, held by Dean.

## BEER MAT STUFFING

The greatest number of standard beer mats ever stuffed into the mouth and held in the teeth is 77 by David Armitage at the Goat Inn, Steeton, Yorkshire, UK, on 1 April 1990.

## BREAK DANCING

Six youngsters comprising the Breakdance team 'Street Machine' led by Brian Numan, set a new world record on 3 May 1986 at Salford, Lancashire, UK, by dancing non-stop for 2 hours, 45 minutes.

## BURNING CANDLE PICTURE

The world's biggest picture made from burning candles was put together by a team of 48 employees of Sandoz Pakistan. The Sandoz company logo was made from 8,157 burning candles (total weight: 814.5 kg [1795.6 lb]) at Serena Hotel Faisalabad, Karachi. The picture measured 223.5 cm x 30.5 cm (88 in x 12 in).

## CHALK DRAWING

Three hundred and sixty volunteers, including employees of Wal-Mart in Hanover, Pennsylvania, USA, took part in a record attempt on 22 February 2004 to sketch and colour in the world's biggest chalk drawing completed within a day. Using a parking lot of Utz Quality Foods, the competitors used 7,200 sticks of chalk to complete the image that stretched to an amazing 2,980 sq m (32,035 sq ft). The drawing shows a hot-air balloon rising over grass – with the sky and sun in the background. In addition in achieving this amazing feat, the volunteers raised more than $2,000 for the Children's Miracle Network, a Utah-based charity that raises funds for 170 children's hospitals throughout North America.

## CHARACTER ARTIST, FASTEST

In 1997, Gero Hilliger from Berlin, Germany, drew a portrait of an unknown person in 6.2 seconds. Gero went on to set a record in 1998 for drawing 384 different portraits in 90 minutes.

On 21 December 2003, while blindfolded, Gero drew a portrait of a person whom he'd never seen before, using his hands to touch the face before drawing it in a world record time of 48.7 seconds.

## CLOWNING MARATHON
During December 1977, clowns Greg Bull and David Grech from Australia clowned around non-stop for 51 hours in Hurtsville, Australia.

## COIN SNATCHING
As the traditional coin snatchers will know, the coins must be snatched using the 'palm down' technique. The greatest number of ten-pence pieces snatched in this fashion is 328 by multi-record holder Dean Gould, achieved in January 1993, in his hometown of Felixstowe, UK.

## COMIC STRIP
The world's biggest comic strip was presented in 1991 in Munich, Germany. Drawn by *Filips*, the comic measured 30 m x 21 m (98.4 ft x 68.9 ft).

## COMPACT DISC FLIPPING
Dean Gould of Felixstowe, UK, flipped a pile of 45 compact discs (not including cases) balanced on the edge of a table 180° before being caught in the same hand with the fingers on top, thumb underneath in a pincer position.

## CUE LIFTING

Jim Mills lifted 24 454-g (16-oz) billiard cues simultaneously holding only the tapered tips, from the vertical to the horizontal (through 90°) at Alfreton Park, Derbyshire, UK, on 13 June 1982. Jim went on to set a new world record by lifting a 624-g (22-oz) cue 1,005 times consecutively by the same method.

## DARTS – USING 6-INCH NAILS

We have all heard stories about the chap who could throw 6-inch nails better than some people could throw darts. Lee Walker from Gravesend, Kent does just that. On 9 September 1984, in a 7-hour, non-stop marathon stint, Lew struck 4,746 6-inch nails in the dartboard achieving a total score of 58,609. The total weight of the nails thrown was 137.4 kg (3 cwt 3 lb).

## DRUMMING (FASTEST)

Mike Mangini, of USA, musician and teacher at Berklee College of Music, in 2004, set a record with 1,180 strokes in one minute. The previous holder, Art Verdi holds the record for the most strokes on a drum in 10 seconds, with 220.

## DRUMMING WITH FEET RECORD

On 22 January 2002, Tim Waterson pushed extreme drumming to a new level when he played an amazing 1,407 beats in 60 seconds in double strokes using only his feet.

## FINGER PAINTING

In July 2000, Xiao Zenglie, a famous finger painter from Pingxiang in the eastern Chinese province of Jiange, painted the world's longest finger painting. Measuring 170 m (557 ft) long, the painting depicts more than 160 historical sites along the Yangtze, China's longest river.

## FOOTBALL SPINNING

The record for spinning a football on one finger is 4 minutes, 21 seconds, established by Raphael Harris (Israel) on 27 October 2000 in Neve Yacov, Jerusalem. He was also the first person to joggle a marathon in Israel (see 'Joggling' in this chapter).

## HIGH WIRE MOTORCYCLING

Karl Traber, the well-known German high-wire artist, set the fastest speed record for riding a motorcycle across a 300-m-long (984-ft-long) wire on 31 May 2003 in Beeskow, Germany. Riding his

KTM GS 250 motorcycle along the wire (from 4.50 m up to 31 m [14.8 ft up to 101.7 ft] above street level), Traber reached a maximum speed of 97 km/h (60.3 mph).

## ICE-SCULPTURE (LONGEST)

It took 20 chefs from four hotels in Malaysia on 30 January 1999 to carve the longest ice carving in the world. Led by art and décor manager Martin Aluk, it took 2 hours to carve a 60.8-m-long (199.47-ft-long) dragon using 100 blocks of ice.

## JOGGLING (3 BALLS WHILE RUNNING)

A 24-hour joggling relay record was set on 3–4 October 2003 by a team of 18 (juggling 3 balls and running), but covering a distance of 176.6828 km (109.8 miles). The event was staged in Hamburg, and organised by Meike Duch and Andreas Lietzow (Germany).

## KARAOKE

The biggest karaoke singing event in history took place on 1 July 1997, when 1.8 million people took part in the event as part of the celebrations surrounding the regaining of Hong Kong to China's rule.

## LEAPING ON (AND OFF) A HORSE

In 1891, Edwin 'Poodles' Hanneford was born in Barnsley, England, the son of a married couple who performed with the Lord John Sanger Circus. Poodles, as he was better known, followed his parent's footsteps and became a part of their circus act, eventually creating a comedy act of his own, which was built upon a foundation of skill as an acrobat and equestrian. During his eventful career, Poodles set a world record by performing 26 continuous running leaps on and off a running horse. Edwin 'Poodles' Hanneford is considered to be the best equestrian clown in history. His style has been widely copied and some of the routines that he created are still performed by Mark Karoly and descendants of the Hanneford family. He died in 1967.

## MAGIC SHOW

In 1983, Wolfgang Karl from Vienna, Austria staged the longest magic show in history. Under his stage name of 'Mr Domino', he performed more than 2,000 magic tricks in 86 hours. Now that's magic!

## MAGIC – VANISHING AND REAPPEARING BALLS

Honolulu magician Monty Witt set a world record

for making 15 sponge balls, each measuring 5.08 cm (2 in), vanish one by one from his hands, then reproducing them all at the same time. Using no gimmicks, just sleight of hand, the magician performed this amazing feat on 10 November 2001.

## MOVIE PRODUCTION

The fastest movie production ever attempted in the world took just 24 hours to make. *Swayamvaram*, a film made for Indian cinema, was produced by veteran Indian film maker Giridharilal L Nagpul and his brother, Ramkishan L Nagpul. Swayamvaram features 12 heroes, 10 heroines and 8 comedians/ villains, and was shot simultaneously. Using a minimum of 10 sets and supported by 15 film units, the movie was jointly directed by 11 directors, each with his own cameraman and editor. At the same time, 5 music directors worked to finish recording the music score.

## MUSICAL PERFORMANCE

The longest musical performance in history started on 5 September 2000 in Halberstadt, Germany, 'As slow as possible' by John Cage is planned to last for 639 years. Once a month the organ will play one tone. The fact that the organ was not constructed at the time the musical performance started was not a problem. The piece begins with a pause, and the first tone was not played until 5 January 2003.

## ONE ARMED JUMPING

Rodolfo Reyes from Spain covered a distance of 10 m (32.8 ft) while jumping on one hand in a time of 20.2 seconds during 2003 in Munich.

## ONE SONG MARATHON

For 63 hours ending on 25 August 1983, the American radio station KFJCFM in Berkeley, California, continually broadcast the 21-year-old rock 'n' roll number 'Louie Louie'. Some 800 different renderings were broadcast, most of them the painful offerings of the station's listeners. The lesser-known performances included 'The Bowl of Slugs' and 'Little Nymph and the Spectonettes'.

## ORCHESTRA OF BICYCLE BELLS

The biggest orchestra of ringing bicycle bells took place on 23 November 2003 at the University of Leipzig, Germany. Conducted and arranged by Professor Jörg Kärger, 500 people played six pieces of music (including a part of Beethoven's 9th symphony) on the unusual instruments; 42 players had to play according to their notes, while the other participants used a sophisticated system showing them who had to ring their bell by projecting signs on a wall.

## ORGAN PLAYING

Multi-talented organist Adrian Wigley, 43, of Brownhills, West Midlands, UK, plays the organ the hard way, with his nose and tongue.

On 31 October 1985, at the Railway Tavern, Brownhills, UK, he played tunes on the organ using only his tongue for a record 2 hours non-stop.

On 23 July 1985, at the Travellers' Rest, Burntwood, West Midlands, UK, Adrian completed a 6-hour, non-stop organ-playing marathon with his nose.

## PAINTING

The World's Largest Painting by one artist was unveiled on World AIDS Day on 1 December 2001 at the North Carolina Museum of Art in Raleigh, North Carolina, USA. The art piece entitled 'Hero' is the work of international artist Eric Waugh, and measures 3,851 sq m (41,400 sq ft). The painting was gently divided up into 41,400 sq ft pieces and sold to raise money for Camp

Heartland, a camp for children affected by HIV and AIDS.

## PIANO PLAYING – UPSIDE DOWN

Club pianist and entertainer Colin 'Fingers' Henry is so versatile he literally plays the piano standing on his head. On 2 August 1987 at the Trustville Holiday Village, Mablethorpe, Lincolnshire, UK, Colin set a new duration record by playing the piano standing on his head for 2 minutes, 15 seconds.

## POLE DANCING

A team of 4 young women broke the world record for marathon pole dancing when they danced on a small stage for 24 hours. Dressed in skimpy union jack bikinis, the women individually danced in 20-minute bursts breaking the previous record held by a team of Americans. Completed by exotic dances Toni-Louise, Jade, Storm and Francesca, the record-breaking feat was in aid of raising money for the Cancer Research Campaign.

## RECORD THROWING

The distance record for throwing a vinyl record is 145.52 m (477.40 ft), which is held by Axel Schulz of Germany.

## ROCK AND ROLL DANCING –
## MOST DULAINES IN A ROW

Synje and Ulf Kohlmann of Germany, a partnership from the dancing group 'Flying Saucers' performed 42 dulaines in a row at the Tummelum, Flensburg, Germany during the record festival held between 7 and 9 July 2000.

## SHAKESPEARE RECITAL

On 15–16 February 2004, more than 150 people of the Wellesley College Shakespeare Society read aloud the complete work of Shakespeare (39 plays, 154 sonnets and poetry) in a record time of 22 hours, 5 minutes.

The solo record is held by Adrian Hilton, of Beaconsfield, Buckinghamshire, who – armed with a host of friends to keep him awake, and with advice from NASA on nutrition and the effects of sleeplessness – took a mammoth 110 hours, 46 minutes – almost five days – to complete the recital on the site of Shakespeare's Globe Theatre, London, as part of the International Shakespeare Festival in 1987.

## SILK PAINTING

A Chinese silk painting entitled 'Zhangzhou Flourishes' holds the record for the longest piece of its kind in the world. Measuring 1,028 m (3,373 ft) in length, and 0.815 m (2.67 ft) wide, the painting was done in a style that combines traditional and modern skills. The work of 182 painters from China, the painting depicts the mountains, historical sites, architectural masterpieces and folk customs of China's Fujian province.

## SINGING MARATHON

Eamonn McGirr from Co. Derry, Ireland, now residing in Loudonville, New York, holds the record for non-stop singing, a record he's held on and off since the 1970s, when he started the record with a time of 132 hours, 45 minutes (5½ days). Beginning on 10 January 1996, Eamonn broke the record live on television on 21 January 1996 during a Telethon to benefit the Centre for the Disabled, the record being exactly 11 days, beating the previous record of 10 days, 22 hours.

## STAIR CLIMBING, ON HANDS

Ex-circus performer Nikolai Novikov broke the record for walking down stairs using only his hands when he 'walked' down 32 flights of stairs (787 steps) in June 2004. A couple of times the daredevil fell, but luckily his team of doctors followed closely behind to pick him up. Novikov, from Russia has practiced handstands since he was four years old, and starved himself for two days in preparation for the stunt.

## STILTS (TALLEST AND HEAVIEST)
The tallest and heaviest stilts ever used for walking measured 15.47 m (50 ft 9 in) in length and weighed 62.14 kg (137 lb) combined. On 14 September 2002, Canadian Doug Hunt took 29 independent steps wearing the stilts to break his previous world record as part of an event to mark the celebrations of the opening of a visitor and tourism centre in Brantford, Canada.

## STILT WALKING MARATHON
In October 2001, Bill 'Stretch' Coleman from Denver, Colorado, USA, walked the Dublin, Ireland, Marathon, a distance of 42.195 km (26 miles, 385 yd) while wearing stilts in a time of 8 hours, 53 minutes, 12 seconds, beating his previous record by one and a half hours.

## STILT WALKING, 1 HOUR/24 HOURS
Zdeněk Jiruše (Czechoslovakia) covered a distance of 122.591 km (76.2 miles) on stilts within 24 hours on 12 June 1992 in Pelhřimov. In 1997, he set another record by walking 9,313 m (5.8 miles) on

stilts within 1 hour.

## STILT MOUNTAIN CLIMBING

Colin Tschida and friend Ryan Hamilton share the record for climbing a mountain while wearing a pair of stilts. During the summer of 2002, the pair set the record when they climbed the 2,195-m-tall (7,200-ft-tall) Harney Peak, in Rapid City, South Dakota, USA, in a time of 2 hours, 20 minutes, while wearing specially made wooden stilts that put their feet 0.6m (2 ft) off the ground.

## STREET ORGAN PLAYING

On 1 September 1994, Jürgen Sinner from Germany began his marathon street organ-playing attempt, and 60 hours later he was officially named the new record holder, beating the previous champion Rolf Becker's record of 48 hours.

## STRIPPING

The longest marathon strip tease ever performed was completed on 2 July 1988 after 72 hours by unemployed actress Delane Balliot, 23, and Newcombe Hunt, 28, in a shop window in Hollywood, California, USA. They both used two large cans of deodorant each and stripped off a record 432 times.

## SYMPHONY CONCERT

The Colorado Springs Philharmonic Orchestra performed pieces from Bach to Beethoven in the world's longest symphony concert. On Friday, 23 May 2003, Denver conductor and promoter Tom Jensen, clad in white tie and tails, lead an insomniac ensemble through a 24-hour concert of popular and classical music in front of a live audience at a Colorado Springs Kings Sooper grocery store.

## TAP DANCING

Dubbed 'Tap-O-Mania' in Stuttgart, Germany, 6,951 dancers took part in the event on 24 May 1998 to become the greatest number of tap dancers ever gathered. It was organised by the New York City Dance School, Stuttgart, and everyone who wanted to take part enjoyed a free tap dancing lesson. The dance was named 'Klicke di Klack'.

## TIGHTROPE SKIPPING

Pedro Carillo (Colombia) managed 1,323 rope-jump skips in 10½ minutes on a high wire 8.2 m (27 ft) above the circus floor at Big Apple Circus, Boston, USA, in 2004. He succeeded in establishing a new world record for the most tightrope skipping jumps in a minute by skipping 134 consecutive skips in 48 seconds.

## TIGHTROPE WALKING

Jay Cochrane, a native of Toronto, Canada, holds several world records for tightrope walking. At the age of 14, Jay joined a circus, soon learning the skills of tightrope walking and aerial cycling. Since then, he's gone on to become the world's greatest aerialists. His records include:

*Longest building-to-building skywalk:* In 2001, Jay skywalked between two 40-storey buildings on opposite sides of the Love River in Kaohsiung, Taiwan, a distance of 667.5m (2,190 ft) in 1 hour, 9 minutes.

*Longest and highest blindfolded skywalk:* Jay Cochrane achieved a world record for skywalking in 1998 when he walked blindfolded 91.4 m (300 ft) above the lights of Las Vegas between the towers of the Flamingo Hilton, a distance of 243.8 m (800 ft).

## UNDERWATER CONCERT

The world's largest underwater concert was held on 8 July 1997 on the floor of the Atlantic Ocean off Florida Keys, USA. Staged by Keys radio station, 650 musicians played at the event in memoriam of Jacques Cousteau. The event also carried the serious message of coral reef preservation.

## VIOLIN PLAYING WHILE RIDING A BICYCLE BACKWARDS!

During 1987, Christian Patzig of Germany rode a bicycle backwards while playing the violin for a distance of 60.45 km (37.56 miles) in a time of 5 hours, 8 minutes. During the record attempt, Christian experienced no problems; however, during a practice session this was not the case. He ran over a policeman!

## WHIP CRACKING

Robert Dante (USA) set the record for most 'cracks of a whip' in a minute on 2 September 2003 at the Dream Circus in Hollywood, Los Angeles (USA). Using a 1.82-m (6-ft) bullwhip made by Australian whip maker Mike Murphy, Dante cracked the whip 203 times.

## YODELLING

The world's largest simultaneous yodel took place on 19 November 2003. Leading global internet company Yahoo! organised the event, bringing 1,773 people together with acclaimed American yodeller Wylie Gustafson leading, trouncing the previous record of 937 that was set a year earlier. The successful record attempt was hosted at Yahoo's headquarters in Sunnyvale, California, USA.

# MENTAL GAMES
# AND COMPETITIONS

## CALCULATION

(Note: In future, no more records for single tasks will be considered. The record categories will be replaced with new records for the fastest time to solve ten tasks in a row [i.e. without a break between the tasks] correctly.)

### ADDITION OF 100 RANDOM SINGLE-DIGIT NUMBERS

This record is for the fastest time an individual adds together 100 single-digit numbers in his/her head. The current world record is 19.23 seconds, held by Alberto Coto of Spain; however, an as yet unconfirmed record of 18.8 seconds was recorded in 2002 by Lam Yee Hin of China.

### CALCULATING THE SQUARE ROOT OF A 6-DIGIT NUMBER

Gert Mittring of Germany broke the world record with a timing of 44.7 seconds at Flensburg, Germany, on 7 July 2000.

### CALENDAR CALCULATING

*One century:* The record is for finding the correct days of the week from 20 random dates from the whole century and 20 dates of the current century must be randomly selected by computer or by taking lottery tickets. The world record with 20 dates was achieved by Matthias Kesselschläger of Germany on 9 November 2003 with a time of 24.94 seconds.

*One year:* The record is for finding the correct days of the week from all 365 or 366 dates from the current year. On 9 November 2003, Matthias Kesselschläger of Germany knocked 4 seconds off the world record with a timing of 218 seconds.

*1600–2000, one minute:* This record is for the greatest number of days of the week correctly identified from random dates between 1 January 1600 and 31 December 2100. Matthias Kesselschläger of Germany broke the record on 9 November 2003 correctly identifying the days of 32 dates in one minute.

## MULTIPLICATION

Johann Martin Zacharias Dase (Germany, 1824–61) multiplied two 20-digit numbers in 6 minutes, two 48-digit numbers in 40 minutes, two 100-digit numbers in 8? hours in 1861. He also multiplied two 8-digit numbers in 54 seconds. These records are historically accepted, although they were not achieved under modern rules.

Jan van Koningsveld, of Germany, broke the

multiplication of an 8-digit number record with a time of 38.1 seconds on 19 March 2004, regaining the record which he had held until 11 January 2004 when it was beaten by Mohammed Seghir Saîd (Algeria) with a time of 45 seconds.

## CHESS

### LARGEST CHESS TOURNAMENT
This tournament was held in Hamburg, Germany, on 24 February 1988 involving 3,616 players from 161 schools. One of the reasons for the large number of participants was the incentive for pupils playing in the tournament. They did not have to go to school.

### MOST OPPONENTS PLAYED BY ONE CHESS PLAYER SIMULTANEOUSLY
The record goes to international chess master Andrew Martin, of UK. On 21 February 2004 at Wellington College, Crowthorne, UK, he played against 321 players simultaneously in a time of 16 hours, 48 minutes, winning 294, drawing 26 and losing just once! During the game play, Andrew walked over 8 km (5 miles) and played more than 7,000 moves.

## MOST OPPONENTS PLAYED BY ONE CHESS PLAYER CONSECUTIVELY

Anna-Maria Botsari, of Greece, played a total of 1,102 opponents consecutively in Kalavrita on 27–28 February 2001. Each player was replaced when a game was completed until a staggering 1,102 games were over.

## CHESS PLAYED BLINDFOLD FROM MEMORY

In 1952, Janos Flesch, of Hungary, played 52 games of chess while blindfold. Relying on memory of the games, he won 31, drew 18 and lost just 3.

## CHESS PROBLEM, LONGEST

Readers who enjoy solving chess problems are invited to try this record-breaking problem, published in 1889 by Otto Titusz Bláthy:

White: King b4, Queen d2, Pawn a5, c2, e6, f2, f4, g2, g5

Black: King c7, Queen a8, Rook e5, Knight g8, h8, Pawn a6, b7, c4, e4, e7, f5, g6, h4. The task to solve? Mate in 257 moves!

## DRAUGHTS PLAYED BLINDFOLD FROM MEMORY

Since 1982, Ton Sijbrands from the Netherlands has

held the record for the most games of draughts played from memory while blindfold. The current record of 22 was achieved on 21 December 2002. Ton won 17, drew 5 and lost none.

## MEMORISING

### *BINARY NUMBERS (30 MINUTES)*
At the 2003 German Memory Championships, Dr Gunther Karsten remembered 3,180 random binary numbers beating his own previous world record of 2,970.

### *FA CUP FACTS*
Creighton Carvello, of Middlesbrough, UK, holds the record for remembering the most sporting facts. The memory champion has remembered more than 4,000 FA Cup facts since the game played in 1872, and can name all 22 players in each and every one. A panel tested him in October 1999 with 50 random questions and calculated that he had beaten the previous world record.

### *MOST DIGITS IN 1 HOUR*
The record for the most numbers recalled after memorising as many digits as possible in 1 hour is

1,920 by Jan Forman (Denmark) at the World Championships 2003 in Kuala Lumpur.

## MOST DIGITS IN 30 MINUTES
The 30-minute record is 1,004 by Astrid Plessl, of Austria.

## NAMES AND FACES
Andi Bell, of UK, holds the record for memorising the most names and faces. Faces are presented in a certain order with corresponding names underneath. They are then presented in a new order without names. Andi was able to mark the names on new sheets, a point being awarded for each correct forename, and one point for each surname. Andi scored 156 at the World Championships in London, UK, beating the previous record of 100 set in 1993 by Jonathon Hancock.

## PI (π)
The most numbers from Pi ever recited without mistakes was achieved in 1995 by Hiroyuki Goto from Japan with an amazing 42,195 digits. Sim Pohann, of Malaysia, managed to recite 67,053 digits of Pi with only 15 errors on 14 April 1999.

## PLAYING CARDS

Dominic O'Brien, of UK, 8-times Memory World Champion, has the record for remembering the most cards using the most packs of cards – 54 packs, reciting a total of 2,808 cards – this is with 8 acceptable mistakes.

The 1-hour record for memorising several packs of cards (52 cards each) was broken at the 2002 Memory World Championships by Andi Bell of UK, with a score of 1,197. No mistakes in a pack of cards score 52 points, one mistake scores 26 points and more than one mistake scores zero points.

Speed record memorising a single pack of cards: Andi Bell, UK, broke the world record in 1998 with a time of 34.03 seconds.

## SPOKEN NUMBERS

Spoken at a rate of one digit every second: The most digits remembered and recited was by Andi Bell (UK) at the 2003 World Championships held in Kuala Lumpur with a total of 140 numbers.

Spoken at a rate of one digit every two seconds: The record for the most digits remembered and recited at a rate of one digit every two seconds was achieved by Dr Gunther Karsten (Germany) during 2000 with a total of 400 numbers.

## WORDS (15 MINUTES)

At the 2002 Memory World Championships, Andi Bell (UK) broke his own four-year-old record when he memorised random words according to the competition rules and scored a world best of 182.

## WRITTEN NUMBERS (5 MINUTES GIVEN)

This is a record that Dominic O'Brien (UK) had dominated since 1993, breaking the records five times, before losing the record to Jan Forman of Denmark at the 2003 World Championships held in Kuala Lumpur. The current record stands at 324 written numbers recalled.

## WORDS OR TEXT

The most impressive feat for learning words – memorising 23,200 words within 72 hours – was reported by Ramón Campayo, of Spain. Unfortunately, there is no official written documentation about his records, so this record cannot be officially accepted, but nevertheless is an amazing achievement.

## RUBIK'S CUBE

*Fastest*

**1 cube:** The best time for restoring the cube in an official championship was 12.11 seconds by Shotaro Makisumi (Japan) at the Caltech Spring Tournament on 3 April 2004. On the same occasion, he set the record for the average from five attempts (where the best one and the slowest one did not count) with 15.38 seconds and the one-handed record with 43.31 seconds.

***Fastest – 2,000 cubes:*** The fastest time for solving 2,000 cubes was achieved by Jess Bonde (Denmark). He solved 2,000 cubes in 22 hours, 16 minutes on 16–17 December 2002 in Århus, Denmark.

***Record time for 4x4x4 cube*** – *Rubik's Revenge:* Masayuki Akimoto (Japan) with 1 minute, 20.16 seconds.

***Record time for 5x5x5 cube:*** David Wesley (Sweden) with 2 minutes, 19.69 seconds.

## RUBIK'S RECORDS (MISCELLANEOUS AND OTHER PUZZLES)

***Rubik's Clock:*** 9.54 seconds by Stefan Pochmann (Germany) at the Open German Championships on 24 April 2004 in Gütersloh.

***Rubik's Magic:*** 2.09 seconds by Jaap Scherphuis

(Netherlands) at the Open German Championships on 24 April 2004 in Gütersloh.

The following records were all achieved at the 2003 World Championships, held in Toronto, Canada:

**Rubik's Master Magic:** 8.22 seconds by Jaap Scherphuis (Netherlands).

**Square-1:** 41.80 seconds by Lars Vandenbergh (Belgium).

**Megaminx:** 2:12.82 minutes by Grant Tegay (USA).

**Pyraminx:** 14.09 seconds by Andy Bellenir (USA).
**3x3 Fusion:** 1:10.96 minutes by Kenneth Brandon (USA).

**Blindfold, most solved:** This record is shared by Geir Ugelstadt of Norway (14 December 1998), and Ralf Laue, of Germany (3 February 2001). They completed three Rubik's cubes in no set time, while blindfolded after studying the 'mixed-up' cubes. The contestants were not allowed to see the cubes while they were being 'mixed up'.

**Blindfold, fastest time:** Dror Vomberg (Israel) 3 minutes, 56 seconds (including memorising).

*Blindfold, fastest time 4x4x4:* Dror Vomberg (Israel) 22 minutes, 35 seconds (including memorising), at the 2003 World Championships held in Toronto, Canada

## ULTRA-SPEED MEMORY
*RANDOM BINARY NUMBERS*
The most number of binary numbers memorised and recalled after they have flashed up on to a screen for:
1 second – 30, Ramón Campayo (Spain),
9 November 2003.
2 seconds – 42, Ramón Campayo (Spain),
9 November 2003.
3 seconds – 48, Ramón Campayo (Spain),
9 November 2003.
1 minute – 154, Lukas Amsüss (Austria),
November 2003.

*RANDOM DECIMAL NUMBERS*
This record is for the greatest number of decimal digits remembered after they have flashed up on a screen for:
1 second – 16, Ramón Campayo (Spain),
9 November 2003
2 seconds – 17, Creighton Carvello (Great Britain)
4 seconds – 22, Gert Mittring (Germany)

13

# STOP PRESS

This chapter has been hastily put together on the eve of printing to include updates to records that appear within the book which have been broken since their original inclusion. We would like to congratulate these record breakers on their recent achievements and, in doing so, reward them with a place within our book.

## CHAPTER 1 – OUTRAGEOUS ACHIEVEMENTS

### FIREWALK, LONGEST
14 firewalkers walked a distance of 250 metres over burning coals on 22 March 2003 at St. Lorenzen, Austria.

### MILK CRATE BALANCING ON HEAD
John Evans, from Heanor, Derbyshire (United Kingdom), holds the record for balancing the most milk crates on his head. On 8 August 2004, John broke this record for The Book of Alternative Records during the Felixstowe Carnival weekend at the carnival arena in Langer Road Park, Felixstowe, UK. He balanced 97 crates on his head.

## CHAPTER 8 – SPORTING RECORDS

*BACKWARDS RUNNING*
On 18 July 2004, Thomas Dold (Germany) set three new records in Meßkirch (Germany): He ran 1,000 m in 3:32.35 min, 1 mile in 5:46.59 min and 2,000 m in 7:13.00 min. Brian Godsey (USA) ran 3,000 m backwards in 11:54 min on 3 July 2004 in Poviglio, Italy.

*PUSHUPS*
On 9 July 2004, Doug Pruden added another record to his impressive list of achievements by completing 5,557 pushups on fists within 3:02:30 hours, at Body Quest Health Club in Edmonton, Canada.

*SWIMMING, LONGEST DISTANCE*
Martin Strel broke his own record when he completed a 4,600-km (2,875-mile) descent of the Yangtze River in 50 days in June–July 2004.

## CHAPTER 12 – MENTAL GAMES & COMPETITIONS

*MEMORISING*
Loredana Feuchter (Romania) set two world records

at the German Memory Championships 2004. She memorised 1,200 decimal digits in 30 minutes as well as 3,390 binary digits in 30 minutes.

## MEMORISING WORDS
Boris–Nikolai Konrad memorised 199 words in 15 minutes at the North German Championships on 4 July 2004.

## RUBIK'S CUBE
Several new world records were established at the US Championships on 10 July 2004, including:

Christopher Hardwick (USA) solved a 4x4x4 cube in 1:12.85 min and a 3x3x3 Rubik's Cube one handed in 25.95 sec.

Shotaro Makisumi (Japan) solved a Rubik's Cube blindfolded in 3:37 minutes.

A few days later, the European Championship was held on 7 - 8 August in Amsterdam, Holland, which saw even more new world records:

Lars Vandenbergh (Belgium) solved a 4x4x4 cube in 1:09:11 min and a 5x5x5 cube in 2:08:45 min.

Stefan Pochman not only solved Rubik's Magic in a world record time of 1.43 sec, he also set the first record for solving a 5x5x5 cube blindfolded in 2:34:36 hours.

Dror Vomberg (Israel) solved a 4x4x4 cube blind-folded in 19:54 minutes. Finally, Kåre Krig (Sweden) solved a Rubik's Cube in 5:44.32 minutes – using only his feet!°

# BECOME A
# RECORD HOLDER

You too could have what it takes to become a record breaker. No matter how great or small, we will consider your record for inclusion in the next edition.

- Can you break one of the records published in this book?
- Are you suggesting a new record category?
- Do you have corrections to the published records?

If the answer to any of the above questions is 'yes', then please contact us via our website: www.alternativerecords.co.uk or send us an e-mail to: editors@alternativerecords.co.uk

# HERE ARE SOME CATEGORIES FOR NEW RECORDS AS A CHALLENGE TO YOU:

Darts: Longest distance from which a bulls-eye was thrown (the dart should remain in the board).

Roller-skating on hands (fastest time for 50 m).
Longest slot-car race (marathon, most hours).

Playing pool underwater (fastest time for potting all 15 balls, which should be made from metal).

Most faces painted by a face painter in a single session.

Underwater Domino toppling (longest/most dominoes used).

Clothes peg pressing (between thumb and index finger) for the longest time (e-mail us for information about the standard peg).

Marathon: Longest dark-ride in an amusement park (5 minutes pause per hour permitted).

Table tennis balls: Most held underwater for ten seconds, using one hand and forearm only.

Hopping: 100-m one-leg hop in the fastest time.

Hopping: The least one-leg hops over the distance of 1 mile.

Furthest distance to flick a pea from a table (table height restrictions apply).

Stapling: The fastest time to staple 100 sets of 2 pages together using 6mm 26/6 staples and manual stapler.

Game marathons: Most hours playing Mikado, mah-jong (for both categories, no record exists so far) or your favourite game.

Running 10 km (or Marathon if you prefer…) wearing frog-man's flippers.

Juggling three objects while blindfolded for the longest time.

World Marathon Fitness Challenge, consisting of:

10-mile treadmill run
Marathon distance on an indoor cycle
(setting 100 kW)